BRITISH MUSEUM PATTERN BOOKS

Ancient Egyptian Designs

Designs

EVA WILSON

Published by British Museum Press

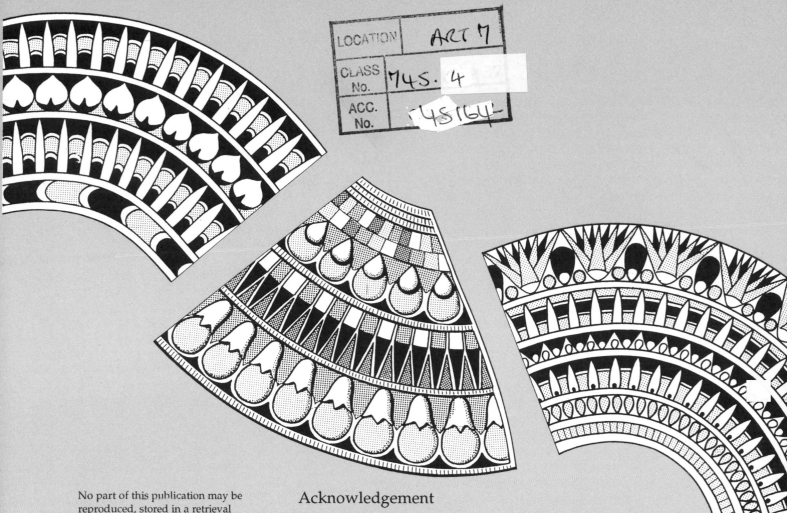

© 1986 Eva Wilson
Sixth impression 1997

Published by
British Museum Press
A division of
The British Museum Company Ltd
46 Bloomsbury Street, London
WC1B 3QQ

British Library Cataloguing in
Publication Data
Wilson, Eva, 1925–
    Ancient Egyptian designs.—(British
    Museum pattern books; v. 3)
    1. Design—Egypt
    2. Decoration and ornament, Ancient
    3. Egypt—Antiquities
    I. Title   II. Series
    745.4'4932   NK1190

    ISBN 0–7141–8061–0

Designed by Roger Davies

Printed in Great Britain
by Page Bros, Norwich

Acknowledgement

I am most grateful to the staff of
the Department of Egyptian
Antiquities in the British Museum
for making available material for
my illustrations and for the use of
their library. I particularly thank
Carol Andrews for her patience
and valuable advice. I am grateful
for permission to publish
drawings of objects in the Petrie
Museum, University College,
London and thank its assistant
curator, Rosalind Hall, for her
help. Finally, I am much indebted
to Ann Hecht for her expert
advice in matters concerning
textiles and weaving.

Contents

Introduction

Ancient Egyptian art is remote in time, its guiding principles were laid down five thousand years ago, and some of its concepts are equally remote and indeed so forbidding that they seem to exclude the intimate and personal. The patterns and designs illustrated here, however, are taken from the decorative motifs which adorn the grand images and which decorate jewellery and humbler objects of daily use. The symbolic reasons why particular motifs were chosen are not relevant to this book, rather it is the manner in which they were used for decorative purposes in different contexts, materials and techniques which is the subject of the illustrations.

The basic nature of the art of the ancient Egyptians changes little from the beginning of the third millennium to the end of the first millennium BC when Egypt became a part of the Roman Empire. In an art which primarily served ritual purposes there was no incentive to innovate.

It may seem an intolerable limitation to illustrate Egyptian decorative art without the colour which is such a striking feature. The use of colour is, however, always secondary to the drawing and is highly conventionalised; although at its best it is used with subtlety. In plant ornament, for instance, colours are generally 'natural', i.e. lotus flowers are blue, leaves green, etc. It is only in the repeat patterns that colour is an integral part of the designs. This is usually done by simply alternating two colours. In painted ceiling patterns, for instance, a shape may be alternately blue or green, the background white or yellow and the outline black or red. Screens of different density have been used in this book to indicate the colour differentiation, but not particular colours, except where this is stated in the captions or notes.

An outline of ancient Egypt

The art and ornament of Egypt must be set against the historical and geographical background from which it developed.

The river Nile has two sources, one in Central Africa, the other in the highlands of Ethiopia. The part of its course which makes up the land of Egypt stretches from the First Cataract at Aswan in the south to the Delta, where the Nile flows into the Mediterranean, a distance of some 750 miles.

All the northern regions of Africa were at one time habitable and covered by grassy plains where Palaeolithic hunters followed the movements of the animals on which they depended. A gradual change in the climate began about 12,000 years ago and led to a decline in rainfall—a process which continues to this day. Desert conditions slowly developed driving the animal and human populations ever further south and east into the valley of the Nile, which became one of the most favourable environments for early man. By about 5000 BC the encroaching deserts had cut off access to the valley from the east and west while the rough waters of the Cataracts in the south and the marshy Delta in the north completed its isolation. This isolation became one of the conditions for the development of the Egyptian civilisation. Another determining factor was the inundation which regularly once a year covered the banks of the river with rich silt.

By this time the population had become Neolithic farmers; their lives were dominated by the annual flood which, together with the stable and sunny climate, ensured good crops provided the necessary irrigation work was carried out—involving a good deal of organised communal labour. All these factors—the isolation, the slow, steady and predictable rhythm of the year's activities, the certainty of crops and the necessity for organised community work, together with the excellent communications afforded by the river—provided the background to the early formation of a state at the end of the fourth millennium BC. Inextricably involved with this process was the growth of a religious outlook which permeated every aspect of Egyptian life. At its most basic level this was a fertility cult founded on the two 'miracles' on which their very lives depended, the daily rising and setting of the sun and the annual rise and fall of the Nile. Figures found in early burials suggest primitive deities in the shape of humans and animals, and there is some evidence that each district had its own god or cult symbols, a trait characteristic of later Egyptian religion.

The interacting elements of geographical setting, natural resources and religious thought created the Egyptian civilisation, characterised by stability, permanence and isolation.

From these ancient times the economy of Egypt was naturally primarily agricultural and the principal crops were corn and flax. The country was rich in animal and bird life and in many other natural resources—flint for tools and weapons, soft steatite for carving, and papyrus, the stems of which were used for building and for the production of fibre as well as paper-making. Useful rocks formed the cliffs and hills which edged the valley and in the Eastern Desert semi-precious stones and metals could be found. Large timber, however, was in short supply and was traded from Western Asia from the earliest times.

The isolation from the outside world was thus not complete and one must assume some contact, either through conquest, migration or trade, with the developing Sumerian city-states along the Tigris and Euphrates rivers. It is likely that it was through such contacts that the idea of writing in pictographs was introduced to Egypt, although the signs themselves took a purely Egyptian form.

In the last millennium of the prehistoric period three distinctive cultures have been identified: the Badarian and Naqada I and II, known as predynastic.

It is with the invention of writing that the historical period begins. The long history of the ancient Egyptian state is divided into a series of thirty-one dynasties (i.e. related kings and queens), a system essentially formulated in the early part of the third century BC by the Egyptian priest Manetho. Supplemented by other more recent evidence, this system provides a very detailed, and probably substantially correct, chronology for a period which begins at about 3100 BC with the unification of Lower and Upper Egypt under one king and ends in 30 BC when Egypt became a province of the Roman Empire.

The dynasties are further grouped together into three 'Kingdoms', i.e. periods of stable and continuous government: the Old Kingdom which lasted for about five hundred years in the third millennium (Third to Sixth Dynasties, c. 2686–2181 BC), the Middle Kingdom which lasted for about three hundred years at the beginning of the second millennium (Eleventh, Twelfth and early Thirteenth Dynasties, c. 2040–1720 BC) and the New Kingdom which lasted for nearly five hundred years in the second half of the second millennium (Eighteenth to Twentieth Dynasties, c. 1567–1085 BC).

The first two dynasties (known as the Archaic Period) saw the unification of the whole of Egypt under one king and the establishment of the basis of Egyptian civilisation. Between the Old and the Middle Kingdoms (First Intermediate Period) there was widespread dissolution and even anarchy, while between the Middle and the New Kingdoms (Second Intermediate Period) a divided Egypt was ruled over by weak kings and by a dynasty of foreigners of Asian origin known as Hyksos. The Late Period, which follows on from the New Kingdom, is divided into ten dynasties (the Twenty-first to Thirtieth) spread over some 750 years and includes rulers of Libyan and Nubian stock, as well as Persian kings. After the conquest by Alexander in 332 BC, Egypt was ruled by kings of Greek descent (the Thirty-first Dynasty of the Ptolemies) and in 30 BC the country became a province of the Roman Empire.

The unification of Egypt some five thousand years ago conferred great benefits on the country. A central administration and a religion which became inextricably linked with royal power controlled the economy. The population increased and

Egypt passed into a fully developed Copper Age. In the following four hundred years or so the basis of the Egyptian civilisation was firmly established: hieroglyphic writing developed, a high standard was reached in craft and industry and the conventions which ruled the art were laid down.

With unification some of the local gods and cult figures emerged as national gods. The falcon Horus—the sky god—became the major god of the state. Others like Ptah, the local god of the capital Memphis, and Re, the sun god, also achieved prominence at this time and retained their importance throughout the Dynastic Period.

The elevation to a higher status of local gods depended on political developments, but other gods continued to be revered in their localities and became part of the immense pantheon of gods who played a part in the religious life of the Egyptians.

Since most of the remains from ancient Egypt come from tombs and temples, one might imagine that the Egyptians were exclusively obsessed with death and burial. It is perhaps more true to say that it was exactly because they so enjoyed life and its sensations that they wished to secure an eternity as similar as possible to life on earth. Ideally, therefore, the Egyptian required a tomb containing his mummy, his inscribed name and carved or painted scenes of food and drink and other desirable services which would be provided for him by magical power. As long as his mummy remained intact his eternal life was assured. It is through these scenes of daily life in tombs and sacred ritual in temples that we have acquired much of our detailed knowledge of this ancient civilisation.

In the beginning of the twenty-seventh century BC, at the beginning of the Old Kingdom and in the reign of Djoser, there was an explosion of innovation apparently due to a single individual of outstanding originality and vision. This was Imhotep, Djoser's architect, a man also involved in many other fields of science and technology. He was the first to develop the Egyptian stone-mason's accumulated skill, in the production of vases, to monumental architectural form. Indeed, before his time, stone had not been used to construct whole buildings. His greatest achievement was the Step Pyramid at Saqqara.

The Old Kingdom lasted for five hundred years and it was during this time that the specifically Egyptian statecraft, religion, ideas and art matured into a mould which was to last essentially unchanged for over two thousand years. This mould can perhaps best be described as monumental, confident and exclusive. Despite foreign trade, influences from abroad were insignificant in Egypt's culture. This cultural self-confidence was closely linked to the all-embracing character of its divine monarchy, which culminated in the Fourth Dynasty with the building of the great pyramids.

Towards the end of the Old Kingdom there was a steady development of a kind of feudalism and decentralisation. This relaxation of central authority led to the collapse of the Old Kingdom. Little is known about the hundred and fifty years or so which followed.

During the three hundred years of the Middle Kingdom, which began with the re-unification of the country under one king in c. 2040 BC, strong rulers curbed the feudal provincialism and returned to a central administration. The frontiers were protected by campaigns against attack from the east of the Delta region, whilst Nubia was conquered in the south. Such foreign contacts served to supply materials for building, arts and crafts. Quarries and mines in the Eastern Desert, Nubia and Sinai were exploited and expeditions to equatorial Africa undertaken. There was extensive trade with Syria and perhaps with Crete. The Middle Kingdom depended for its security on strong leadership, and, when during the Thirteenth Dynasty c. 1720 there was no strong successor, the country again lapsed into decentralisation. This was the beginning of the 150 years known as the Second Intermediate Period.

The anarchy and confusion during the First Intermediate Period was not repeated; the high officials in the various provinces carried on the administration as before despite a rapid succession of weak kings. When the Hyksos took over control of the country they did not impose their Asian culture on Egypt but assumed the style of Egyptian royalty and patronised Egyptian art and literature. They did, however, introduce the extensive use of bronze—instead of copper—for tools and weapons. Bronze had already been the common material for such purposes in Asia since before the Middle Kingdom.

It was understandably unacceptable to the Egyptians to be ruled by foreigners and it was a noble Theban family who, in the middle of the seventeenth century BC, over a period of a hundred years managed to break their supremacy and unite Egypt again under an Egyptian king.

This New Kingdom lasted for five hundred years and Egypt was ruled for half of this period by one dynasty, the Eighteenth. During the Old and Middle Kingdoms Egypt had been content with its own frontiers and had pursued a traditional isolationist policy, deeply and fundamentally linked to its beliefs and self-sufficient culture. With the beginning of the New Kingdom a great change took place. While the frontiers were strengthened and secured, a militant and aggressive foreign policy extended Egyptian power far beyond their own territory. Hostile powers in western Asia were turned into satellites and allies and in the south, Nubia was conquered and controlled. Egypt became a major world power, her empire sustained not only by military might but also by great wealth of gold. For the first time Egypt became a member of the international community and came into contact—particularly through trade—with other societies with different political and religious systems of a similar status to her own.

At the beginning of the New Kingdom there was a renaissance in the arts based on and inspired by the best of Middle Kingdom art, together with many new ideas, techniques and influences.

The fortunes of Egypt reached a high point with the reign of Amenophis III (c. 1417–1379 BC). The empire extended from the Sudan to the borders of the Hittite Empire in western Asia and was secure and at peace. At home great prosperity allowed the king to engage in extensive building activities. Among the monuments of this period the temple at Luxor, dedicated to Amen-Re, was particularly outstanding. Amun had already during the Middle Kingdom become the state god of Thebes, the capital. As a result of the Theban kings' victory over the Hyksos kings, his status had been much enhanced. When merged with Re, the sun god, as Amen-Re, he became a super-god to which other gods became subordinate. Amen-Re was not merely a national god but was worshipped throughout the Egyptian Empire as the creator of the world.

The introduction of new ideas also had a deeply disturbing effect on the political and religious stability in Egypt. It may also have paved the way for the curious episode of Akhenaten (Amenophis IV) and his religion of sun-worship. Considerable speculation has arisen about the nature of the man and his religion. There seems to be only a small theological difference between the ideas behind the cult of Amun and that of Aten, the sun-disc, which had already been introduced as a cult subsidiary to that of Amen-Re. Akhenaten made Aten the central object of worship as a new super-god, while at the same time persecuting the cult of Amun and all other gods. As a result he met with considerable resistance to such sudden change, not only from the priests of Amun, but also from most of the establishment. Akhenaten built a new city for himself at El-Amarna, halfway between Thebes and Memphis in Middle Egypt. It is here that his distinctive taste in art was given free reign and can be seen in one of the few sites where secular building has been recovered in excavation. This distinctive style was not a radical departure from the traditional approaches to art in Egypt, but was rather a shift in emphasis from the static and monumental to a more naturalistic and mannered treatment of the traditional motifs.

Akhenaten's preoccupation with his new religion and his lack of interest in the politics of empire led to a certain neglect of Egypt's allies abroad, hard pressed by the growing power of the Hittites. On Akhenaten's death in 1362 BC, after a reign of only seventeen years, the city of Amarna was abandoned, government returned to Thebes and the cult of Amun was re-established during the short reign of Tutankhamun who died, still a youth, in 1352 BC. Horemheb, a general who had been an adviser to Tutankhamun now took over and, sharing the administrative power with the priests of Amun, he proceeded to restore stability within Egypt and control over the empire abroad. Meanwhile all memory of Akhenaten and his religion was officially forgotten and eradicated from the contemporary records.

The Nineteenth Dynasty of the Ramesside family from the Delta was founded in 1320 BC. For over a hundred years Egypt's power was restored under efficient rulers who also engaged in large monumental building works at home. However, the major migrations of people from the coasts and islands of Asia Minor brought about near collapse at the end of the dynasty. During the last dynasty of the New Kingdom (the Twentieth) Egypt again managed for a short time to draw together the extensive regions of its empire under the strong and prosperous government of Ramesses III, but eventually the Asian empire was lost.

Egypt was not alone in suffering at this time; she shared the fate of her allies and enemies—the Hittite Empire, the independent city-states of Syria and Palestine, Minoan Crete and Mycenean Greece—who were all swept away or suppressed by nomads from the steppes of Asia in westward migrations. The international community of which Egypt had been part collapsed and declined. The classical world which gradually emerged from the ruins was of a different character and Egypt no longer played a central role.

After the end of the New Kingdom, ruling power was held by kings of Libyan origin, sometimes in rival dynasties and often in conflict with the High-Priests of Amun in Thebes.

This fragmentation was halted when a prince from Nubia gained control over most of the country in the middle of the eighth century BC and introduced a firm rule. This dynasty (the Twenty-fifth, known as Kushite) came from a native line of rulers who had preserved many Egyptian customs and who worshipped Amun. In the seventh century BC, however, Egypt suffered attacks from the Assyrian kings. The Nubian kings retired defeated to their homeland in the south and another dynasty was established in Egypt (the Twenty-sixth, known as Saite) by princes from Sais, the final period of true Egyptian independence. There was a last flowering of art in Egypt, again harking back to the ancient art of the Old and Middle Kingdoms.

Egypt now became the last major civilisation to enter the Iron Age, although the metal had been available there in small quantities for centuries. In the Near East it had been in common use already for more than seven hundred years. It was not until the Roman period in Egypt, at the end of the first millennium BC, that iron was extensively used.

Egypt's isolation could not be reinstated, and once again developments abroad intruded when in 525 BC Egypt became a satrapy of the Persian Empire. In 332 BC Alexander the Great conquered Egypt which then became a province of his Macedonian Empire. During the dissolution which followed Alexander's death in 323 BC, his satrap in Egypt, Ptolemy Lagus, became king and established a dynasty, known as the Ptolemaic. From now on the administration was organised on Greek lines; Greek became the official language and new ideas and tastes in art were introduced from the Greek world. Finally, this energetic dynasty succumbed, as had many before, to weakness and dissolution and in 30 BC Egypt became a province of Rome.

Conventions in Egyptian art

Certain features in the representation of figures and scenes make Egyptian art instantly recognisable. Although generally outside the scope of this book, it may nevertheless be of interest to examine very briefly some of the conventions which guided the Egyptian artists and formed their images. The conventions sprang from fundamental attitudes to the world and from the role art played in the social and religious life of the people. This subject has exercised the minds of many art historians and is discussed in great depth by H. Schäfer, *Principles of Egyptian Art*, Oxford 1974.

The art is essentially two-dimensional and its basis is drawing—even three-dimensional sculptures began as sketches drawn on the sides of square blocks of stone. The Egyptians sought to express the essential nature of objects, not the impressions of a moment or a view from a particular angle. In translating solid forms into two dimensions the typical and enduring aspects of the subject was identified and the accidental excluded; an object was represented in terms of what was known rather than what was observed. Several views of the object were therefore combined to make up images of great clarity and simplicity. The word *aspective* has been coined to describe this mode of representation. Some examples of this approach are shown in plates 2 and 5. The drawings in plate 5 TOP LEFT of a jug standing in a basin illustrate three solutions to the problem of showing the known shape of both vessels without the high sides of the basin obscuring the shape of the jug.

There is no attempt to create the illusion of space. The scene in plate 4 represents a man, a palm and a pond in a spatial relationship which is purely two-dimensional, yet perfectly clear. In a group of objects in the horizontal plane, like the spread of offerings in plate 3, those nearest are shown at the bottom while those further away are placed higher up. This approach also leads to the drawing of a king much larger than a courtier, since he is a personage of much greater importance.

Artists were trained to draw standard motifs; the human figure, animals, plants and other subjects according to conventions. A canon of proportion was developed which ensured the harmonious assemblage of standardised parts. Instances where the grid on which the designs were drawn survive and reveal how the system worked. (For further information on the canon of proportion see W. H. Peck, *Drawings from Ancient Egypt*, London 1978.)

The majority of the decorative details from the wall-paintings and minor objects (which are the source of many patterns illustrated here) are, however, more informal and were created without recourse to the strict canons. While many plant and animal motifs were originally based on observations from nature, their conventionalised forms, which were repeated for thousands of years, can only be used to identify actual species with great caution despite their convincingly realistic appearance. Thus the lotus motif is obviously based on a real plant, but the lily motif has defied all attempts to identify a particular plant species, on which it could have been based, and it appears to be a conventionalised motif based on several plant elements. (Some of the most important decorative motifs are discussed below.) A flock of birds illustrated in plate 6 demonstrates how a conventional image may be used to give the impression of a study from nature: all the birds have identical bodies, but are arranged facing right and left at different angles and have wings attached to their outline in different positions.

The Egyptians believed in the actual independent life of images, which was the reason for covering their tomb walls with pictures of the many things the dead might need in the afterlife. There has been speculation that some deviations from the natural forms and attributes of animals may have been deliberate and motivated by a reluctance to let loose dangerous beasts in the tombs—this kind of double-thinking would not be at all foreign to the Egyptian mind.

Painting

The walls and ceilings of the tombs were decorated with painting throughout the Dynastic Period, as were domestic buildings made of unbaked mud-brick. The paint—a distemper—was applied to designs in low relief or to flat, plastered surfaces. The craftsman-painters were professionals, usually working as members of a team. Their training was rigorous and based on conventions which provided them with great technical skill in the use of the strictly defined motifs and methods of representation. Within these limits the excellence of much of their work demonstrates that this training did not exclude the development of the individual artistic genius.

The design was first drawn on the wall. It must be presumed that there were small preliminary drawings which were transferred to the large wall spaces using square grids based on the canon of proportion for the standard human figure and other important motifs. Examples of these grids can be seen on unfinished paintings. If the design was to be in relief, the sculptor followed this outline drawing. The paint added further detail and was applied by yet another member of the team. Flat murals would also have been completed by a number of painters, each carrying out a particular aspect of the design.

Brushes were made from the *Juncus* rush plant. The cut end of the stalk was chewed to make a fine brush capable of producing both thin and thick lines. Bigger brushes were made from other plant materials. The pigment was mostly mineral—chalk, iron oxides, copper compounds, ochre etc—which was ground and mixed with a binding agent such as plant gum. The paint was applied by the tempera method and was diluted with size, gum or egg. A varnish of natural resin sometimes protected the painted surface.

This is not the place to describe the Egyptian method of writing except to point out the close relationship between writing, painting and drawing. The form of many hieroglyphs and the conventional form of the same motif when used in decoration was often the same. The name 'scribe' was applied to both the clerk and the artist; they were initially trained together and used the same brushes and paints in their work. Images were used to support written texts and *vice versa*. An example of the unification symbol in plate **35** TOP illustrates this point. The lily representing Upper Egypt and the papyrus representing Lower Egypt are tied round the lung-and-trachea sign meaning 'to unite'; together they mean the unification of Upper and Lower Egypt. In this example two figures are seen tightening the knot made by the plant stems, a dramatic effect which greatly enhances the message.

Jewellery

The role of jewellery as adornment is obvious, but the fundamental purpose of jewellery in ancient Egypt was as amulets—charms tied to vulnerable parts of the body to protect the wearer from mysterious and hostile forces.

The broad collar is perhaps the most striking piece of jewellery worn by the ancient Egyptians; it is pictured so often that it may almost be regarded as an item of dress. The collar is first encountered on statues and reliefs from the early Old Kingdom. Collars were made of several rows of beads and pendants which were held in position by broad terminals. Heavy jewelled collars would have a counterpoise at the back (**49** TOP). Beads of stone, the colours of which were seen as symbolic, were preferred—carnelian the colour of blood, green turquoise the colour of growing vegetation and lapis lazuli the colour of the sky. Gold was a symbol of the sun. Claws, horns and tusks of animals and sea shells were also thought to contain magic virtues. Magic signs and hieroglyphs were fashioned into pendants or were included in the designs.

Very rich jewellery was worn only by the king and the royal family, the court and temple priests; otherwise such pieces were conferred as decorations, rewards and gifts to favoured subjects. The court and temples were therefore the main employers of the goldsmiths and most of the gold which was produced, as well as that levied in taxes, was held in the king's treasury.

Gold was found in large quantities in Egypt, particularly in its metallic form as granules in the sand and gravel of the desert; it was also mined from veins in quartz rock. Egyptian gold naturally contains varying amounts of silver which can produce a paler-coloured metal (known as electrum) or a white metal (known in Egypt as white gold). The naturally occurring variations were used by the jewellers, and in the New Kingdom such alloys were probably achieved artificially. Pure silver was imported.

The stones which were set in gold or electrum—rarely in silver—were primarily carnelian from the Eastern Desert, turquoise mined from veins in sandstone outcrops in the Sinai and lapis lazuli which was imported and originated in Afghanistan. Other stones found in Egypt included jasper, garnet and amethyst. Cheaper substitutes for these gems were transparent calcite or rock-crystal backed by coloured cement in inlays or by alkaline glazes and frits (powdered glass).

The chief goldsmiths had received a basic training as scribes before specialising in the decorative arts. The work was carried out by a team of craftsmen, each with his own special skills. Tools and techniques were extremely simple. The furnace was a pottery bowl on a stand filled with charcoal, the blowpipe a reed with a clay nozzle. Sufficiently high temperatures could be achieved by these simple means to allow a hard solder of naturally occurring alloys to melt—natron probably being used as flux. It is suggested that gold work was also joined by colloidal hard soldering (C. Aldred, *Jewels of the Pharaohs*, London 1971, pp. 99–100). In order to melt a large mass of metal, several blowpipes were brought to bear on the fire beneath a clay crucible, but by the time of the New Kingdom, a blast furnace worked with leather bellows had been introduced.

Gold and silver were hammered and beaten into leaf by polished pebbles held in the hand. Embossing and chasing were done with hardwood, bone or metal punches over cores of pottery, wood, stone or metal. Abrasive stones and crushed quartz sand were used for polishing. In the absence of shears, trimming was done with chisels.

The most characteristic technique employed in Egyptian jewellery was cloisonné. Designs were outlined in strips of metal, which were placed on edge and soldered onto base plates to form cells. The cells were filled with coloured inlays of stone or other material. This technique is known from the early Old Kingdom, but it became particularly popular in the New Kingdom; the gaudy effect of many objects in Tutankhamun's tomb is due to the use of gold cloisonné (**38**, **43** CENTRE, **60**, **61** RIGHT, **62**, **63** CENTRE and BOTTOM LEFT, **65** LEFT).

Basketry, weaving and dress

Basketry is the oldest domestic craft of the Nile valley. Examples are known from as early as the Neolithic Period of the fifth millennium BC. The materials used were plant fibres of all kinds: reeds palm ribs and heavy grasses for the foundations and palm leaves, halfa grass and flax for the sewing and twining. Most baskets were made in the coiled technique and differ little from those made today (**19**, **20** BOTTOM, **21** BOTTOM). Some were produced by twining, which could result in a slightly open fabric used for strainers and bags, as well as a closer fabric for chair seats and mats etc (**21** TOP). The patterns reflect the techniques and consist typically of triangles and chevrons.

Plaiting and weaving would have developed alongside basketry, the same materials being used in both crafts. Linen from the First Dynasty (*c.* 3000 BC) has been found to have a warp count of 65 and a weft count of 50 threads per centimetre, a rather finer weave than that of a modern handkerchief. Cloth could be woven in large pieces; from the beginning of the second millennium there are examples of rolls of cloth some eighteen metres in length.

The use of linen is well documented, not only by the finds of cloth, but also in the depiction in wall-paintings and reliefs of the harvesting, preparation, spinning and weaving of flax. Most of the Egyptians shown in paintings wear white linen clothes, sometimes pleated and sometimes sheer to the point of transparency. Most of the cloth found in tombs are wrappings and bandages from mummies and lengths of cloth; a few actual garments do, however, survive. From the evidence of statuary and wall-paintings it would seem that Egyptian garments were very simply tailored and consisted mainly of rectangular pieces wrapped round the body in different ways according to fashion. Men wore a 'kilt'—a plain or pleated strip of fabric of varying width wrapped round the hips and tied in front (**3**, **4**, **53**). They also sometimes wore a shirt or tunic with or without attached sleeves (**70**). Women wore a close-fitting dress with shoulder straps, which may have been made up of a piece of cloth sewn together to form a tube, or wrapped round the body like a sarong (**65**, **69**). Both sexes wore simple cloaks fastened at the neck.

Spinning and plying was done on a spindle weighted by a whorl. The illustration from a tomb in plate **69** shows the two threads drawn up from separate pots and plyed. The woman apparently holds another spindle behind her back. The same painting also shows a horizontal, or ground, loom—the earliest type in Egypt—drawn in the Egyptian convention. The warp on this loom was stretched between two beams, secured in the ground by a peg at each corner. The chain of threads at the top probably represents laze threads, which enabled the weaver to disentangle the warps at this point. One of the two cross-sticks would be in the heddle-rod. The long stick held by the weaver on the right is probably a 'sword' used for beating down the weft. No shuttle is shown. The woven cloth has a pronounced selvage on one side.

A representation of an upright loom is also shown in plate **69**. Looms of this type had been in use in neighbouring Asia since the beginning of the third millennium and were perhaps one of the products of new technology introduced to Egypt during the Hyksos Period in the seventeenth and sixteenth centuries BC. On this type of loom the warp is stretched between beams fitted into an upright frame. This representation shows little detail—the warp, for instance, is not differentiated from the cloth—but it can be seen that the two weavers sit in front of the loom holding sword-beaters. The upright loom did not replace the ground loom, but it was more flexible, and while the same type of plain cloth could be produced as on a ground loom, particularly in larger sizes, it could also be used for tapestry weave.

Linen is difficult to dye colourfast and the knowledge of mordants—chemicals which fix the dye permanently to the fibre—was not introduced in Egypt until the end of the Dynastic Period. The wearing of white garments was therefore perhaps a necessity rather than a matter of choice. Rare examples of linen cloth dyed in monochrome colours are found, but it is thought that these would have been fugitive (i.e. not colourfast); there is no evidence that such cloth was frequently worn.

Apart from simple striped patterns on clothes depicted in tombs and on statuary, there is no evidence of clothes with woven or embroidered coloured patterns worn by Egyptians before the New Kingdom. Representations of patterned garments of earlier dates may have been ornamented with fine pleating, beads, feathers or patchwork—or they may show clothes of dyed or painted leather or fabrics woven from other plant fibres like grasses in natural or dyed colours.

Wool was not much used in Egypt, save perhaps for rough cloaks. This may have been because of religious taboos against wool garments, or more simply because the native sheep were hairy, rather like goats, and produced no wool. Egypt's eastern neighbours, however, commonly used wool, which is much easier to dye than linen. Figures represented in colour-patterned garments are therefore usually identified as slaves or foreigners. For instance, the Semitic travellers illustrated in plate **72** TOP may be wearing woollen clothes.

In the New Kingdom a few patterned textiles appear in the tombs. Most are self-patterned in stripes, but for colour-patterning several techniques occur—embroidery, tapestry and warp-face weaving. Their sudden appearance, and certain foreign elements in their design, suggest that some of these techniques came from abroad at a time when influences from Egypt's extensive empire introduced many new ideas and techniques.

The textiles in the tomb of Tutankhamun illustrate the range and quality of the patterned fabrics available at this time. The textiles themselves are in a very poor state of preservation, but an impressive variety of techniques can be identi-fied—simple striped weaves, tapestry-woven tunics and gloves (**63** TOP), belts and braids in warp-face weave (**61** LEFT, **68** LEFT, **71**) and embroidery in outline and chain stitch (**70** BOTTOM), as well as a cloth embroidered in beads. The colours are difficult to determine; analysis has revealed the use of madder and indigo (perhaps Egyptian woad) and other dye-stuffs, but the colours were not fixed and the fabrics could not have been washable. (See also notes to 70–71.)

The so-called 'Girdle of Ramesses III' (**68** LEFT) is in a much better state of preservation and allows a closer study of the warp-face weaving technique. The design on the five-metre long and tapering strap is of two lengthwise stripes separated by a plain white field. The main motif is the hieroglyphic sign *ankh* meaning 'life'. There has been a good deal of controversy associated with this object: it has been suggested that it was made by tablet-weaving, but it is now generally agreed that this is a warp-face weave, produced on a simple ground loom like that described above on p. 15. (See also note to 68.)

Other patterned fabrics from the Old Kingdom onwards include matting, hang-ings, canopies and sails—all often depicted on the walls of the tombs. The mater-ials used to produce such fabrics can only be guessed at—woven plant fibres or leather could be painted, embroidered, appliquéd or decorated with beads etc.

Silk was first introduced into Egypt under Greek influence during the Ptolemaic Period towards the end of the first millennium BC and cotton was brought in during the Roman Period.

The use of beads to produce patterns on cloth is particularly associated with a design of lozenges found in many contexts in wall-paintings and statuary from the Old Kingdom onwards on garments, hangings, canopies, cushions etc (**64**, **65** TOP LEFT). The beads were either woven into the cloth or stitched on to it, or (as on the figure illustrated here in plate **65**) the beads were made up into a separate net worn over a dress of plain fabric.

A unique dress of tubular beads from the Fifth Dynasty (*c.* 2494–2345 BC) was discovered in the Qau Southern Cemetery and is now in the *Petrie Museum, University College*, London (UC 17743). Blue and black cylinder beads make up a wide-meshed net, measuring about 51 × 57 cm, with green ring-beads at each crossing point. There is a bead fringe and a string of shells at the bottom and towards the top two caps, 4.3 cm in diameter, which were worn over the breasts. This was probably the costume of a dancer, the shells rattling as she moved.

Pottery and glazed composition ware (faience)

The earliest pottery in Egypt dates from the predynastic Badarian Period at the end of the fifth millennium BC. This pottery is well made and hand raised; its burnished surface sometimes finely ribbed but otherwise without decoration. In the following Naqada I Period, some pottery was decorated with white or cream painted designs on a burnished red body (8–11). Geometric patterns are most common, but some have representations of animals, particularly hippopotamus (1 and 10). The geometric designs are simple, but not entirely unsophisticated. The designs inside bowls (8–9) show variations in the division of a circle into different numbers of equal parts, but also, intriguingly, of unequal divisions. In the design in plate 9 BOTTOM RIGHT a numerical element is introduced with the sequence of one to four triangles contained in the unequal arms of the cross.

Some of these simple patterns also occur elsewhere in the Near East in similar forms. Whether or not this indicates direct contact between cultures, or indeed migrations of populations, is a matter of controversy. Patterns like these could easily develop spontaneously among different peoples. It has been suggested that the cross-hatched patterns on pottery derive from basketry or weaving and the triangle or chevron is a common basket pattern in Egypt as elsewhere in the world (18–23). Since spindle whorls have been found in Egypt already in the fifth millennium BC, woven materials as well as plaited and twined mats and ropes were other obvious sources for patterns at this early period.

A very different type of pottery was produced in the Naqada II Period towards the end of the fourth millennium BC. These were large bulbous vessels in a buff ware with highly stylised boats, animals, figures and plants painted in red and distributed in a haphazard fashion over the surface. Some of these motifs are illustrated in plates 16 and 17. The motifs together create a picture of some ritual activity in a marshy river environment.

With the beginning of the Dynastic Period, native decorated pottery disappears and all domestic pottery is undecorated and utilitarian for the next fifteen hundred years. During this time decorated pottery from abroad reached Egypt through trade, perhaps mainly as containers for trade goods. The use of the potter's wheel, however, which was known in Mesopotamia as early as the fourth millennium, was introduced in Egypt in the middle of the third millennium BC.

It is only in the Eighteenth Dynasty of the New Kingdom that some painted Egyptian pottery again briefly appears in the record. These are sometimes very large vessels painted predominantly in blue on a cream slip with designs of flowers and garlands (52–53). This fashion did not last long and, by the end of the dynasty, native pottery again became quite plain. Pottery was not decorated in Egypt again until Roman times, nor was any glazed pottery produced in Egypt until then.

Glazed and decorated ware was, however, produced on a body other than clay—commonly, but incorrectly, known as faience. The core on which the glaze was applied could be solid quartz, steatite (a kind of soapstone) or a composition of quartz sand or rock crystal ground to a fine powder and probably bound with a weak solution of natron or salt. This mass could be worked with the fingers, or shaped in open pottery moulds. The object was coated with an alkali glaze, made by heating together sand (i.e. silica with lime impurities) and natron or plant ash. The glaze was fused to the body by heating. The most common colours of the glaze were shades of green and blue produced by the addition of copper compounds. In the New Kingdom other colours were added.

Throughout the Dynastic Period glazed stones and composition were extensively used for beads, scarabs, amulets and small sculpture. The ease with which the composition material could be moulded allowed such objects to be mass produced. The multi-coloured elements of the floral collars from the Amarna period are examples of mass-produced articles in this material (**48–50**, **51** BOTTOM). The designs on glazed bowls, chalices and bottles from the New Kingdom are among the most attractive in Egyptian art. The strict discipline of the conventions are relaxed a little to allow a more informal and joyful expression of the traditional motifs (**40** RIGHT, **42** BOTTOM RIGHT, **43** LEFT, **82–85**).

Scarab seals

The ancient Egyptians had no locks: lumps of clay impressed with the owner's seal were attached to linen strips or flax cords which tied the handles or knobs of doors and containers to discourage theft. Such seals are known from the Archaic Period onwards and are found in very large numbers. The earliest seals are of many shapes: some are cylindrical, round or ridge-backed, others have animals crouched on their backs (**88–89**). All were perforated and would have been carried on a string. The seals of ordinary people were very small, typically between one and three centimetres long. The seals of kings and the rich were much larger and more elaborately mounted, sometimes in rings.

From the Middle Kingdom the majority of seals are in the form of a scarab beetle with the seal design on the underside (**90**). The scarab, or dung beetle, was sacred from prehistoric times. There are a number of beetles in this group, the largest and most powerful of which is *Scarabaeus sacer* L. (**90** TOP LEFT). The idea of venerating the scarab seems to have arisen from its habits. These beetles live off dung and carrion: *Scarabaeus sacer* makes a perfectly round ball, larger than himself, from the dung and pushes it along, hiding it finally in the ground. This was seen as a symbol of the earth and the passage of the sun from sunrise to sunset. It is this beetle which is most often portrayed in the seals, although the details vary and other species may be represented. However, it must not be presumed that a specific beetle was necessarily represented, in this as in other instances, realistic potrayal was not always intended.

The engraved seal designs most frequently consist of names or mottoes in hieroglyphs or they feature other signs and symbols which reflect another function of these objects as amulets. Some seals, however, have abstract designs or portray plants, animals or humans. The variety of designs, fitted into the small, oval or egg-shaped field of the scarab is truly astonishing (**91–100**). It is possible to distinguish typically early (**91**) or late (**100**) designs, but most were used over very long periods in very similar forms.

Some important motifs

The Egyptians relied on inspiration from the natural world for decorative motifs. The main motifs were developed from plants which also played an important role in their lives. While originally based on observations in nature, they took on conventionalised forms which show only minor variations throughout the Dynastic Period.

The *papyrus* no longer grows in Egypt but was in the past abundant in the wetlands. It is still found in the upper reaches of the White Nile and in Central Africa. *Cyperus papyrus* L. (**28** LEFT) can reach a height of five metres; it has a leafless stem of triangular cross-section with leaf-sheaths at the base and flowers carried on long fronds in a large umbel at the top. The papyrus grew wild in dense groves but was also extensively cultivated. It was a most useful plant: the root and stem base was eaten, the stems, tied in bundles, were made into rafts and boats and were also used in house construction. The rind of the stem was turned into fibres from which baskets, mats, rope etc, were woven and the writing material, which bears its name, was made from layers of the pith cut in thin strips.

Some examples of the conventional forms of the papyrus motif are illustrated in plates **28–31**. The features by which the motif can be recognised are the swelling at the base of the stem which is surrounded by leaf-sheaths; in three-dimensional representations the triangular cross-section of the stem is often indicated. The open umbel, or head, is triangular and, when in colour, the fronds are green with red tips. The length of the sepals, or outer leaves, of the umbel is no more than half that of the fronds. A papyrus grove, which in nature has a ragged appearance with the large heads swaying on their slender stems, was rigidly stylised to ribbed or striped designs topped by heads and buds, often in regular sequence. It is only during the brief Amarna period that a more naturalistic effect was attempted (**29**).

The *lotus* motif was based on two distinctive species of water-lilies. The white lotus *Nymphaea lotus* L. (**40** LEFT) is distinguished by the rounded shape of the flower and of the individual petals. The calyx leaves have pronounced ribs and the edge of the round leaf is scalloped. The blue lotus *Nymphaea caerulea Sav.* (**42** LEFT) has narrower petals and a more pointed, triangular outline. The calyx leaves are spotted and the round leaf has a smooth edge. The petals of the lotus close at night and re-open with the sun in the morning. It became a symbol of the sun and the resurgence of life.

The motif based on the blue lotus is by far the most common. In its conventionalised form the spots on the calyx leaves are often not represented and its character as a water-lily ignored. It is even sometimes shown on a long, straight stem (**42** RIGHT CENTRE).

Both lotus motifs occur abundantly on wall-paintings: growing in water, carried as a spray or held to the nose—the blue lotus had a pleasant smell (**3**, **41** TOP RIGHT, **42** TOP, **43** BOTTOM). They are frequent motifs on jewellery, glazed bowls and small domestic objects (**43–44**, **76–77**, **79** TOP, **82–85**, **87** TOP and LEFT). They are shown in representations of garlands and tall flower arrangements together with the other flowers and fruit (**45**).

The *garland* became an important motif. Very elaborate garlands of lotus flowers, petals and other plants and fruit have been found on many mummies, and such garlands were represented in painting on statues and wall-paintings as well as in jewellery (**46**, **48–51**). The garland motif was also adapted to decorative borders both on objects and on walls and ceilings (**47**, **56–7**). The most common arrangement is a sequence of alternate lotus flowers and buds, seen in endless variation but rarely deviating from this formula. The looped or arcaded stems on some of these borders, and the spiral framework of many repeat patterns on tomb ceilings (**58–59**), together with the lotus and bud sequence, became one of the motifs which Egypt contributed to the art of the Mediterranean world.

It should perhaps be noted that the Indian pink lotus *Nelumbo nucifera* was only introduced into Egypt late in the first millennium BC and does not appear as a motif in Egyptian art before the Roman Period.

There is no agreement on whether or not the *spiral scroll* was indeed a separate Egyptian invention. Trading contact with Crete in the Middle Kingdom (*c.* 2040–1720 BC), which brought pottery to Egypt decorated with scroll motifs, has been cited as a possible source for this ornament. However, the use of highly developed scroll patterns on scarab seals of the type illustrated in plates **92–94** from the First Intermediate Period (*c.* 2181–2040 BC) suggest that it was an indigenous Egyptian motif. Other influences from Minoan art can perhaps be seen in the interlocking structure of some ceiling patterns which show a departure from the Egyptian tendency to make up repeat patterns by lining up the elements of the design in rows and borders (**25**, **74** LEFT and CENTRE).

The origin of the *lily* motif, seen in its typical form in plates **38–39**, has given rise to much speculation. There is no single plant which can convincingly be identified as its model, although several have been suggested. The lily became the heraldic plant of Upper Egypt, known as the 'Lily of the South'. It was, however, preceded, in this role by other plants, particularly by a sedge-like motif (**34** TOP, **36** TOP and BOTTOM). Such representatives from the Old Kingdom, and other motifs made up of curved plant elements (**37**), appear to have contributed, not only to the conventional form of the lily motif, but also to the palmette-like design with which it is often associated (**39**). The lily and the Egyptian palmette would seem to be variations on the same motif and can often not be distinguished from each other (**67** BOTTOM). The name 'palmette'—which suggests palms, is something of a misnomer. This is another motif which, together with the lotus and the scroll, reached the Near East during the time of the Egyptian Empire in the New Kingdom and became part of the repertoire of motifs in the Classical Mediterranean world.

These versatile and beautiful motifs, which were repeated over immensely long periods in Dynastic Egypt, in relative isolation from the rest of the world, and in a spirit of self-sufficiency became a fertile basis for rapid development in the hands of craftsmen with different attitudes. Some of the most important decorative motifs in the world of art were thus developed from the Egyptian lotus, plant scroll and palmette.

Notes on the Designs

1 Design on predynastic bowl. Diameter 19.4 cm. Mesaeed. Naqada I Period, mid-4th millennium BC. *Boston Museum of Fine Art.* (On pottery see p. 17.)

2 TOP LEFT Detail from the funerary papyrus of the priest Hor Akhmim. Ptolemaic Period (*c.* 300 BC). (10479) *British Museum.* TOP RIGHT Detail of painting on a model house. No provenance. Early Middle Kingdom (*c.* 2000 BC). *Ägyptologischen Institutes der Universität Heidelberg.* CENTRE Detail from stela. Helwan. 1st Dynasty (*c.* 3100–2890 BC). BOTTOM Painting of a ground loom in the tomb of Khety, no. 17, Beni Hasan. 11th Dynasty, Middle Kingdom (*c.* 2020 BC). (Drawing after an old copy, it may therefore not be correct in all details. On conventions and aspective representation see p. 12.)

3 Detail from a wall painting in the tomb of Nakht, no. 52, Thebes. 18th Dynasty, New Kingdom (*c.* 1425–1417 BC). (On conventions and aspective representation see p. 12.)

4 Detail from wall-painting in the tomb of Irinufer, Deir el-Medina, no. 290, Thebes. 20th Dynasty, New Kingdom (*c.* 1200–1085 BC). (On conventions and aspective representation see p. 12.)

5 TOP LEFT Jugs and basins after H. Schäfer, *Principles of Egyptian Art*, Oxford 1974, fig. 93. TOP RIGHT Detail from wall-painting in the romb of Nebamun and Ipuky, no. 181, Thebes. 18th Dynasty, New Kingdom (*c.* 1417–1362 BC). BOTTOM Detail from the funerary papyrus of the scribe Nakht. 18th–19th Dynasties, New Kingdom (*c.* 1350–1300 BC). (10471) *British Museum.* (On conventions and aspective representation see p. 12.)

6 Detail from wall-painting in the tomb of Neferherenptah, Saqqara. 5th Dynasty, Old Kingdom (*c.* 2350). (On conventions see p. 12.)

7 TOP Detail from a painted floor in the palace of El-Amarna. 18th Dynasty, New Kingdom (*c.* 1379–1362 BC). *Cairo Museum.* CENTRE Detail from a wall-painting in the tomb of Sennedjem, Deir el-Medina, no. 1, Thebes. 19th Dynasty, New Kingdom (1320–1200 BC). BOTTOM Design on a chest of wood, veneered in ivory and painted in black and red. Tomb of Tutankhamun, Valley of the Kings. 18th Dynasty, New Kingdom (*c.* 1361–1352 BC). *Cairo Museum.*

8 Predynastic pottery, mainly from Naqada after W. M. F. Petrie, *Prehistoric Egypt*, London 1917. TOP LEFT pl. xiii:37, diameter 11 cm; TOP RIGHT pl. xii:24, diameter 26 cm; CENTRE pl. xi:22, 10.5 cm; BOTTOM LEFT pl. x:8, diameter 10.5 cm; BOTTOM RIGHT pl. x:9, diameter 14.5 cm. Naqada I Period, mid-4th millennium BC. (On pottery see p. 17.)

9 Predynastic pottery from Naqada after W. M. F. Petrie and J. E. Quibell, *Naqada and Ballas*, London 1896. TOP LEFT pl. xxviii:34, diameter 19.8 cm; TOP RIGHT pl. xxviii:48, diameter 16.2 cm; BOTTOM LEFT pl. xxviii:46, diameter 16.8 cm; BOTTOM RIGHT pl. xxviii:36, diameter 21 cm. Naqada I Period, mid-4th millennium BC (On pottery see p. 17.)

10 Predynastic pottery. TOP LEFT height 21 cm, no provenance. (58199) *British Museum.* TOP RIGHT after *Naqada and Ballas* (see note to 9) pl. xxix:76, height 31.2 cm. BOTTOM LEFT (58200); and BOTTOM RIGHT (53882), no provenance. *British Museum.* Naqada I Period. Mid-4th millennium BC. (On pottery see p. 17.)

11 Predynastic pottery from Naqada. After *Naqada and Ballas* (see note to 9). TOP LEFT pl. xxix:79, height 17.4 cm; BOTTOM RIGHT pl. xxix:52, height 11.4 cm. After *Prehistoric Egypt* (see note to 8). TOP RIGHT pl. xiv:43, height 22.8 cm; BOTTOM LEFT pl. xi:16, height 6.3 cm. Naqada I Period. Mid-4th millennium BC. (On pottery see p. 17.)

12 Predynastic slate palettes: TOP length 14.5 cm, ?Thebes (67664). BOTTOM LEFT length

10.5 cm, ?Thebes (67658). BOTTOM RIGHT length 5.5 cm, ?Thebes (67657). *British Museum.* Ivory combs: after *Prehistoric Egypt* (see note to 8) LEFT pl. xxix:2, length 8.3 cm; CENTRE pl. xxix:12, length 8.6 cm. RIGHT after *Naqada and Ballas* (see note to 9) pl. lxiv:85, length 12.7 cm. Naqada I Period. Mid-4th millennium BC.

13 Predynastic slate palettes. TOP length 18.5 cm (57948); CENTRE length 23 cm (37913); BOTTOM length 17 cm (57947). No provenance. *British Museum.*

14 Predynastic slate palettes. TOP length 8.9 cm. Naqada, grave 1562. *Ashmolean Museum*, Oxford. BOTTOM length 22.4 cm. No provenance. (36368) *British Museum.*

15 Predynastic slate palettes: TOP length 15 cm. (65238); BOTTOM length 13 cm. Gebelein. (20910) *British Museum.* Ivory combs: TOP length 12.2 cm. Naqada, grave 1562. *Ashmolean Museum*, Oxford; BOTTOM after *Naqada and Ballas* (see note to 9) pl. lxiii:63, length 15.3 cm.

16 The painted motifs are taken from various vessels. For a discussion of the identification of the tree motif with the banana tree *Ensete edule*, see V. Täckholm and M. Drar, *Flora of Egypt* iii, 1954, p. 523ff. Drawing of the plant after J. Bruce, *Travels to Discover the Sources of the Nile . . .*, Edinburgh 1790. Naqada II Period, late 4th millennium BC. (On pottery see p. 17.)

17 Motifs from vessels in the *British Museum* (36238) and *Medelhavsmuseet*, Stockholm (10.306). Naqada II Period, late 4th millennium BC. (On pottery see p. 17.)

18 From a wall painting in the Mastaba of Seshemnefer III, Giza. 5th Dynasty, Old Kingdom (c. 2400 BC). *University Tübingen.*

19 Oval basket with lid. Length about 19 cm. No provenance. 18th Dynasty, New Kingdom (1567–1320 BC). (5395) *British Museum.* The main colour is a reddish brown with the pattern in black and light buff. (On basketry see p. 14.)

20 TOP Basket painted on the inner coffin of Nofri, El-Bersha. Early Middle Kingdom (c. 2040 BC). CENTRE Oval basket lid. Length 26 cm. No provenance (55300). BOTTOM Oval basket. Length approx. 23 cm. No provenance (6312). Probably New Kingdom (c. 1567–1085 BC). *British Museum.* These baskets are in a poor condition and the patterns have been reconstructed. (On basketry see p. 14.)

21 TOP Detail of a circular basketry mat. Diameter 22 cm. (21885) BELOW Detail of a slightly conical basket lid. Diameter 24 cm, height 4.5 cm. (6329). Probably New Kingdom (c. 1567–1085 BC). *British Museum.* (On basketry see p. 14.)

22–23 Representations of baskets taken from wall paintings in the tombs of Rekhmire, no. 100, Thebes and Nakht, no. 52, Thebes. 18th Dynasty, New Kingdom (c. 1475–1420 BC).

24 TOP Ceiling pattern in the tomb of Amenemhat, no. 2, Beni Hasan. 12 Dynasty (c. 1971–1928 BC). LEFT and CENTRE Border and patterns from wall painting in tomb 3121, Saqqara. BOTTOM Painted panelling on facade of tomb 3505, Saqqara. 1st Dynasty, (c. 3100–2890 BC).

25 Painted ceiling patterns. TOP and CENTRE in tomb of Wahka II, Qaw el-Kebir. 12th Dynasty, Middle Kingdom (c. 1842–1797 BC). BOTTOM in tomb of Hepdjefa, Asyut. 12th Dynasty, Middle Kingdom (c. 1971–1928 BC). The grids on which the designs are constructed have been added as an aid to the modern designer who may wish to draw patterns of this type. The original gridwork is not known in these examples. (On painting see p. 13.)

26 Painted ceiling patterns. TOP in tomb of Nebamun, no. 90, Thebes. 18th Dynasty, New Kingdom (c. 1425–1379 BC). CENTRE in tomb of Neferhotep, no. 49, Thebes. 18th Dynasty, New Kingdom (c. 1417–1362 BC). BOTTOM in tomb of Wahka II, Qaw el-Kebir. 12th Dynasty,

Middle Kingdom (c. 1842–1797 BC). (On grids see note to **25**, on painting see p. 13.)

27 Painted ceiling patterns. TOP and CENTRE in tomb of Wahka II, Qaw el-Kebir. 12th Dynasty, Middle Kingdom (c. 1842–1797 BC). BOTTOM in tomb of Nebamun, no. 90, Thebes. 18th Dynasty, New Kingdom (c. 1425–1379 BC). (On grids see note to **25**, on painting see p. 13.)

28 LEFT *Cyperus papyrus* L. CENTRE and RIGHT Details from a painted relief in the Chapel of Amen-Re, temple of Sethos I, Abydos. 19th Dynasty, New Kingdom (c. 1318–1304 BC). BOTTOM Detail from bed, carved in wood and covered with gold and further embellished by chasing. Tomb of Tutankhamun, Valley of the Kings, 18th Dynasty, New Kingdom (c. 1361–1352 BC). *Cairo Museum.* (On the papyrus motif see pp. 18–19.)

29 TOP LEFT Detail of marsh scene in low relief in the tomb of Mereruka, Saqqara. 6th Dynasty, Old Kingdom (c. 2340 BC). An ichneumon (a type of mongoose) is stalking a bird among the papyrus. RIGHT Detail from wall-painting in the tomb of Amenemhat, no. 82, Thebes. 18th Dynasty, New Kingdom (c. 1504–1450 BC). BOTTOM Detail of wall-painting from El-Amarna. 18th Dynasty, New Kingdom (c. 1379–1362 BC). (On the papyrus motif see pp. 18–19.)

30 From LEFT to RIGHT: engaged pillar from Djoser's Step Pyramid at Saqqara. 3rd Dynasty, Old Kingdom (c. 2650 BC); pillar from the funerary temple of Nyuserre, Abusir. 5th Dynasty, Old Kingdom (c. 2430 BC); pillar from the tomb of Panehesy, El-Amarna. 18th Dynasty, New Kingdom (c. 1379–1362 BC); pillar from Karnak. 18th Dynasty, New Kingdom (c. 1504–1450 BC).

31 From LEFT to RIGHT: detail from a wall-painting in the tomb of Panehesy, El-Amarna. 18th Dynasty, New Kingdom (c. 1379–1362 BC); detail from a wall-painting in the tomb of Ipuy, no. 217, Thebes. 19th

Dynasty, New Kingdom) (c. 1304–1237 BC); another detail from a wall-painting in the tomb of Panehesy; detail from a relief in the temple of Sethos I, Abydos. 19th Dynasty, New Kingdom (c. 1318–1304 BC); detail from the temple at Semna. 18th Dynasty, New Kingdom (c. 1504–1450 BC).

32 TOP LEFT Detail from relief in the temple of Queen Hatshepsut at Deir el-Bahri. 18th Dynasty, New Kingdom (c. 1503–1482 BC). BOTTOM LEFT Detail from wall-painting in the tomb of Sennedjem, Deir el-Medina, no. 1, Thebes. 19th Dynasty, New Kingdom (c. 1320–1200 BC). CENTRE Pendant in glazed composition from Helwan. 1st dynasty (c. 3100–2890 BC). The pendant is damaged and has been reconstructed in the drawing. TOP RIGHT Detail from a slate palette from ?Abydos. Proto-dynastic c. 3100. The palette is in two fragments, the lower part is in the *British Museum* (20791), the upper part in the *Ashmolean Museum*, Oxford. Damaged parts are reconstructed in the drawing. BOTTOM Design on the back of a seal. 4.3 × 2.6 cm. (48953) *British Museum.*

33 From the LEFT: wooden pillar in the cabin of the boat from the pit beside Cheops' pyramid, Giza. 4th Dynasty, Old Kingdom (c. 2570 BC); stone pillar from the funerary temple of Sahure, Abusir. 5th Dynasty, Old Kingdom (c. 2470 BC); detail in low relief from the tomb of Vizir Ramose, no. 55, Thebes. 18th Dynasty, New Kingdom (c. 1379–1362 BC); stone pillar from temple at Soleb. 18th Dynasty, New Kingdom (c. 1425–1417 BC).

34 TOP LEFT and RIGHT details of reliefs on the thrones of statues of Chephren. 4th Dynasty, Old Kingdom (c. 2550 BC) *Cairo Museum;* TOP CENTRE Detail from the throne of a statue of Mycerinus. 4th Dynasty, Old Kingdom. *Museum of Fine Art Boston;* BOTTOM Detail on the throne of a statue of Amenophis III, Thebes. 18th Dynasty, New

Kingdom (*c.* 1400 BC). *British Museum.*

35 LEFT and RIGHT The heraldic plants, the Lily of the South and the Papyrus of the North in high relief on two pillars in the temple of Amen-Re, Karnak. 18th Dynasty, New Kingdom (*c.* 1504–1450 BC). TOP Engraved design on the throne of a statue of Sesostris I, Tanis. 12th Dynasty, Middle Kingdom (*c.* 1971–1928 BC) *State Museum,* Berlin. BOTTOM Inlaid design on a wooden bow-fronted box from the tomb of Tutankhamun, Valley of the Kings. 18th Dynasty, New Kingdom (*c.* 1361–1352 BC). *Cairo Museum.*

36 TOP LEFT Plants from a hunting scene in the funerary temple of Sahure, Abusir. 5th Dynasty, Old Kingdom (*c.* 2470 BC) TOP CENTRE RIGHT Hieroglyph on stela of Wepemnofret, Giza. 4th Dynasty, Old Kingdom (*c.* 2570 BC). *Museum of Anthropology of California.* TOP RIGHT Detail in relief on pillar at Karnak 12th Dynasty, Middle Kingdom (*c.* 1971–1928 BC). *Cairo Museum.* CENTRE Design of head-band from the tomb of princess Khnumet at Dahshur. 12th Dynasty, Middle Kingdom (*c.* 1929–1895 BC). The head-band is of gold with inlays of red, blue and green. *Cairo Museum.* BOTTOM Design on the base of a statue of Tuthmosis III, Karnak. 18th Dynasty, New Kingdom (*c.* 1504–1450 BC). *Cairo Museum.* (On the lily motif see pp. 19–20.)

37 TOP LEFT *Chrysanthemum coronarium* L. TOP RIGHT Carved ivory box. Diameter approx. 5.5 cm. Helwan. 1st Dynasty (*c.* 3100–2890 BC). CENTRE Design on the head-band on a painted statue of Nofret. Mid-4th Dynasty, Old Kingdom (*c.* 2610 BC) *Cairo Museum.* BOTTOM LEFT Reconstructed design from a shrine depicted in the funerary temple of Sahure, Abusir. 5th Dynasty, Old Kingdom (*c.* 2470 BC). BOTTOM CENTRE ABOVE Gold disc from head-band in the tomb of an unknown princess at Giza. Diameter 7.8 cm. 4th Dynasty, Old Kingdom (*c.* 2613–2494 BC).

Cairo Museum. BELOW Gold disc from head-band inlaid with red and green stones from the tomb of princess Sit-Hathor-Iunet at Lahun. Diameter approx. 2.6 cm. 12th Dynasty, Middle Kingdom (*c.* 1842–1797 BC). *Cairo Museum.* BOTTOM RIGHT Design on a disc from a head-band in a tomb at Giza. 5th Dynasty (*c.* 2494–2345 BC). After W. Stevenson Smith, *The Art and Architecture of Ancient Egypt,* Harmondsworth 1958, (fig. 21b).

38 TOP Detail of gold cloisonné from a breast ornament. CENTRE The designs of three bands in cloisonné on the handle of a dagger. BOTTOM Detail of the design, painted in black and red on an alabaster model boat. Tomb of Tutankhamun, Valley of the Kings, 18th Dynasty, New Kingdom (*c.* 1361–1352 BC). *Cairo Museum.* (On cloisonné see p. 14, on the lily motif see pp. 19–20.)

39 LEFT and RIGHT Details of embossed and chased designs in gold on a dagger and sheaths. CENTRE Papyrus burnisher in ivory. Length 16.5 cm. Tomb of Tutankhamun, Valley of the Kings. 18th Dynasty, New Kingdom (*c.* 1361–1352 BC). *Cairo Museum.* (On the lily/palmette motif see pp. 19–20.)

40 LEFT The white lotus, *Nymphaea lotus* L. RIGHT TOP Painted design inside a glazed bowl. Diameter 9.3 cm. 18th Dynasty, New Kingdom (*c.* 1400–1320 BC). *Musées Royaux d'Art et Histoire,* Brussels. BOTTOM Glazed chalice. Height 12 cm. Grave S55, Aniba. 19th Dynasty, New Kingdom (*c.* 1320–1200 BC). (On glazed composition see pp. 17–18, on the lotus motif see p. 19.)

41 TOP LEFT Figure with white lotus flowers attached to a head-dress on a wall-painting in the tomb of Djehutyhotpe, no 2, Deir el-Bersha. 12th Dynasty, Middle Kingdom (*c.* 1971–1878 BC). TOP RIGHT Detail in low relief. Mastaba of Akhethotpe, Saqqara. 5th Dynasty, Old Kingdom (*c.* 2400–2345 BC). BOTTOM

Alabaster lamp in the shape of a white lotus plant. Height 28 cm. Tomb of Tutankhamun, Valley of the Kings. 18th Dynasty, New Kingdom (*c.* 1361–1352 BC). *Cairo Museum.*

42 LEFT The blue lotus, *Nymphaea caerulea* Sav. RIGHT TOP Detail from a wall-painting in the tomb of Kenamun, no. 93. Thebes. 18th Dynasty, New Kingdom (*c.* 1450–1425 BC). CENTRE Detail from a breast ornament in gold with inlays. Tomb of Tutankhamun, Valley of the Kings. 18th Dynasty, New Kingdom (*c.* 1361–1352 BC). *Cairo Museum.* BOTTOM Glazed chalice. Tomb D115, Abydos. Height 14 cm. 18th Dynasty, New Kingdom (*c.* 1504–1379 BC). *Museum of Fine Arts,* Boston. (On the lotus motif see p. 19.)

43 TOP Blue glazed hippopotamus with black painted decoration. Length 20 cm. Tomb of Senbi, Meir. 12th Dynasty, Middle Kingdom (*c.* 1991–1895 BC). *Metropolitan Museum of Art,* New York. CENTRE Design of the counterpoise of a breast ornament in gold, electrum and inlaid lapis lazuli, coloured stones and glass. Height 6.2 cm. Tomb of Tutankhamun, Valley of the Kings. 18th Dynasty, New Kingdom (*c.* 1361–1352 BC). *Cairo Museum.* LEFT Glazed amphora with painted design. Height 14.5 cm. 18th Dynasty, New Kingdom (*c.* 1567–1320 BC). *Metropolitan Museum of Art,* New York. RIGHT Wooden cosmetic spoon with lid in the shape of a lotus flower with two buds and topped by a mandrake fruit. Length 27.5 cm. No provenance (5966). 18th Dynasty, New Kingdom (*c.* 1567–1320 BC). *British Museum.* BOTTOM Detail from wall painting in the tomb of Khnumhotpe, no. 3, Beni Hasan. 12th dynasty, Middle Kingdom (*c.* 1900 BC).

44 LEFT and RIGHT Steering oars in wood from model boats found in tombs of the Middle Kingdom (*c.* 2040–1786 BC), Lengths 13–17 cm. *Cairo Museum.* CENTRE TOP Design in low relief in the chapel of Akhethotpe, Saqqara. 5th

Dynasty, Old Kingdom (*c.* 2400–2345 BC). CENTRE Pendant in gold cloisonné with inlay of blue and green glass and carnelian. Approximately 2 cm across. ?Thebes. (3077) Middle Kingdom (*c.* 1900–1800 BC). *British Museum.* BOTTOM ABOVE Frieze in high relief on the base of a kohl pot illustrated by Prisse d'Avennes, *Histoire de L'Art Egyptien,* Atlas I, 1878, pl. L. BELOW Frieze in low relief in the tomb of Ptahhotpe, Saqqara. 5th Dynasty, Old Kingdom (*c.* 2400–2345 BC).

45 From LEFT to RIGHT Cosmetic spoon of wood with lid. The ornament is carved and inlaid with green paste and bone. Height 30.7 cm. Memphis. (5965) New Kingdom (*c.* 1300 BC). *British Museum.* Design in low relief in the tomb of Ptahhotpe, Saqqara. 5th Dynasty, Old Kingdom (*c.* 2400–2345 BC). Part of the design on the back of the throne in the tomb of Tutankhamun, Valley of the Kings. 18th Dynasty, New Kingdom (*c.* 1361–1352 BC). The wooden throne is covered in sheets of gold into which are set coloured glass, glazed inlays and stone. The colours are several shades of blue, green and red. The drawing does not show the true distribution of these colours; it merely attempts to clarify the elements and motifs in the design. *Cairo Museum.* Detail from a wall painting in the tomb of Amenemhat, no. 2, Beni Hasan. 12th Dynasty, Middle Kingdom (*c.* 1971–1928 BC). Design, incised and painted, on the lid of an alabaster casket in the tomb of Tutankhamun. *Cairo Museum.*

46 Reconstruction of method of stitching petals and leaves together in strands for garlands (after Schweinfurth in V. Täckholm *Faraos Blomster,* 1969, p. 113). CENTRE LEFT Detail of the painted collar on the bust of Nefertiti. 18th Dynasty, New Kingdom ((*c.* 1379–1362 BC). *Berlin Museum.* RIGHT Detail of the design of a garland on an ivory chest in the tomb of Tutankhamun, Valley of the Kings. 18th Dynasty, New

Kingdom (*c.* 1361–1352 BC). *Cairo Museum.* BOTTOM LEFT Detail of the design of a collar worn by Tutankhamun on the throne in his tomb. Gold with coloured inlays. *Cairo Museum.* RIGHT Detail of a collar on a wall painting in the temple of Sethos I, Abydos. 19th Dynasty, New Kingdom (*c.* 1318–1304 BC). (On the garland motif see p. 19.)

47 TOP Design from a breast ornament in gold with coloured inlay. LEFT Sequence of designs on the base of an alabaster model boat. RIGHT Sequence of designs on an ivory chest. Tomb of Tutankhamun, Valley of the Kings. 18th Dynasty, New Kingdom (*c.* 1361–1352 BC). *Cairo Museum.*

48 The glazed beads and terminals for this collar were found during excavation at El-Amarna. (59334) The stringing is a reconstruction based on other examples. 18th Dynasty, New Kingdom (*c.* 1379–1362 BC). *British Museum.* (On glazed composition see pp. 17–18.)

49 Detail from a wall-painting in the tomb of Nebamun and Ipuky, no. 181, Thebes. 18th Dynasty, New Kingdom (*c.* 1417–1362 BC). BELOW Detail of collar of glazed composition beads. El Amarna. 18th Dynasty, New Kingdom (*c.* 1350 BC). *Metropolitan Museum of Art*, New York. (On glazed composition see pp. 17–18.)

50 LEFT Sequence of beads for a collar as found at El-Amarna. These and other examples of beads of this type RIGHT are from the collections in the *British Museum* and the *Petrie Museum, University College, London* (UC. 24392, 24393, 23636, 34392). Plain beads are either blue or green. These beads were mass-produced using clay moulds. (On glazed composition see pp. 17–18.)

51 Necklaces with beads and pendants of a variety of materials are common throughout the Dynastic Period TOP Detail of necklace. Length of pendant 2.2 cm. (3076) New Kingdom (*c.* 1500–1200 BC) *British Museum.* CENTRE LEFT Cloisonné pendant. Length 4.8 cm. Tomb of Queen

Mereret, Dahshur. 12th Dynasty, Middle Kingdom (*c.* 1800 BC). *Cairo Museum.* The design on the pendant represents a collar of petals with a lotus flower at the top. CENTRE RIGHT: group of gold pendants, left: the eyes and thorax of the fly are embossed and pierced with slots and soldered to the back plate which forms the wings. Length 9 cm. Tomb of Queen Ahhotpe, Western Thebes. 17th Dynasty, New Kingdom (*c.* 1567 BC). Top: one of many identical gold birds probably attached to a wig. Embossed gold foil soldered to a back plate. Height 1.1 cm. Tomb of Princess Khnumet, Dahshur. 12th Dynasty, Middle Kingdom (*c.* 1929–1895 BC). Both in *Cairo Museum.* Below: fish of gold from Haraga. Length 4 cm. 12th Dynasty, Middle Kingdom (*c.* 1900–1800 BC). *Royal Scottish Museum*, Edinburgh. Right: fly of embossed and chased gold foil. (59116) Length 2 cm. New Kingdom (*c.* 1550–1300 BC). *British Museum.* BOTTOM Necklace with jasmin flowers and buds in glazed composition beads. New Kingdom (*c.* 1400–1200 BC) *Berlin Museum.* (On jewellery see pp. 13–14.)

52 Wine jar from El-Amarna. (56841) Height 76 cm. 18th Dynasty, New Kingdom (*c.* 1379–1362 BC). *British Museum.* (On pottery see p. 17.)

53 LEFT Jar from Amarna house P49. Height 36 cm. 18th Dynasty, New Kingdom (*c.* 1379–1362 BC). *Ägyptisches Museum*, Berlin. RIGHT Detail from wall-painting in the tomb of Ipuy, no. 217, Thebes. 19th Dynasty, New Kingdom (*c.* 1304–1237 BC). (On pottery see p. 17.)

54 From LEFT to RIGHT: Representation in low relief of pillar in the tomb of Khunes, Zawiyet el-Amwat. 6th Dynasty, Old Kingdom (*c.* 2345–2181 BC) (after Prisse d'Avennes, *Histoire de L'Art Égyptien*, Atlas I, 1878, pl. xv). Pillar in the tomb of Khety, no. 17, Beni Hasan. 11th Dynasty, Middle Kingdom (*c.* 2020 BC). The pillar is painted in blue and red. (after L. Borchardt, *Die*

Ägyptische Pflanzensäule, Berlin 1897, fig. 10). Detail of pillar. Middle Kingdom (*c.* 2040–1786 BC). (After Borchardt, fig. 11.) Pillar from Karnak. 18th Dynasty, New Kingdom (*c.* 1504–1450 BC). (After Prisse d'Avennes).

55 From LEFT to RIGHT: Pillar in the tomb of Ptahshepses, Abusir 5th dynasty, Old Kingdom (*c.* 2430 BC), (after Borchardt, fig. 9 (see note to 54).) Pillar in low relief in the tomb of Mereruka, Saqqara. 6th dynasty, Old Kingdom (*c.* 2340 BC). Pillar in low relief. Saqqara. 5th Dynasty, Old Kingdom (*c.* 2494–2345 BC). (After Prisse d'Avennes, pl. xvii, see note to 54.) Pillar from a model house in the tomb of Meketre, Deir el-Bahri, no. 280, Thebes. 11th dynasty, Middle Kingdom (*c.* 2000 BC). Pillar in low relief in the tomb of Vizier Ramose, no. 55, Thebes. 18th dynasty, New Kingdom (*c.* 1379–1362 BC).

56 TOP Mosaic frieze from an architectural fragment. Palace of Ramesses III at Tell el-Yahudiyah. (38273) *British Museum.* 20th Dynasty, New Kingdom ((*c.* 1170 BC). The roundels are white and grey with yellow centres. Like the petals they are moulded in composition material. The other pieces are cut into irregular shapes of the same material in red and green. The mosaic is set in black matrix. Diameter of the largest roundel is 5.2 cm. BOTTOM Frieze of moulded pieces of glazed composition. Height 7.7 cm. Shibin el-Kom. 20th Dynasty, New Kingdom (*c.* 1198–1166 BC). *Cairo Museum.* The lotus shapes are blue and green while the others have blue bunches of grapes alternating with red fan-like motifs on a yellow background. (On glazed composition see pp. 17–18.)

57 Painted border patterns. The colours—red, several shades of blue and green, yellow and white—are normally those of the flowers and fruit illustrated. The screens serve to show how they are distributed. All the designs are taken from wall paintings in tombs, from the TOP: tomb of

Pairy, no. 139, Thebes; tomb of Nebamun, no. 90, Thebes and tomb of Amenhotpe-si-se, no. 75, Thebes. 18th Dynasty, New Kingdom (*c.* 1425–1379 BC) and tomb of Nespaneferhor no. 68, Thebes, 21st Dynasty (*c.* 1000 BC).

58 Painted ceiling patterns in tombs of the 18th Dynasty, New Kingdom (*c.* 1504–1348 BC). From the TOP: tomb of Amenemhat, no. 82, Thebes, tomb of Neferhotep, no. 49, Thebes and tomb of Nebamun, no. 90, Thebes. (On gridwork see note to 25; on painting see p. 13, on the scroll motif see p. 19.)

59 Painted ceiling patterns in the tomb of Pediamenopet, no. 33, Thebes. Early 26th Dynasty (*c.* 660 BC), (after Prisse d'Avennes, pl. xxxi, see note to 54). (On gridwork see note to 25; on painting see p. 13, on the scroll motif see p. 19.)

60 Breast ornament in gold cloisonné. Width 13 cm. The sun-god carries the sun's disc on his head with the *ankh* (life) and *shen* (infinity) signs in his talons. Tomb of Tutankhamun, Valley of the Kings, 18th Dynasty, New Kingdom (*c.* 1361–1352 BC). *Cairo Museum.* (On cloisonné see p. 14.)

61 LEFT Textile no. 1045. After G. M. Crowfoot and N. de G. Davies, 'The Tunic of Tutankhamun', *The Journal of Egyptian Archaeology*, vol. 27, 1941. The band is 39 cm long and 5.5–8.5 cm wide, it is woven in a warp-face weave with s-spun linen thread. The colours are difficult to distinguish but may have been red (shown here as black), blue (screen) and yellow (white). CENTRE Representation of an ostrich feather fan on a carved and gilded wooden shield. RIGHT Wing or tail feather pattern in gold cloisonné on a coffin. Tomb of Tutankhamun, Valley of the Kings. 18th Dynasty, New Kingdom (*c.* 1361–1352 BC). *Cairo Museum.* (On warp-face weave see note to 70–71 and p. 16, on cloisonné see p. 14.)

62 LEFT Sequence of patterns on the Second State Chariot in

Tutankhamun's tomb. The wooden body of the chariot is covered with a sheet of gold with bands of embossed designs and inlays of coloured glass in blue, red and green. RIGHT TOP Detail of the breast feather pattern on a gilded wooden statue of the god Ptah, shown wrapped in a feathered costume. CENTRE Pattern on the sheath of a dagger. The dark blue feathers have embossed central lobes of gold while the background is striped in red and green. BOTTOM This highly stylised version of the feather pattern decorates the wings of a scarab on a breast ornament. Tomb of Tutankhamun, Valley of the Kings. 18th Dynasty, New Kingdom (*c*. 1361–1352 BC). *Cairo Museum*. (On cloisonné see p. 14.)

63 LEFT TOP The reconstructed pattern on a linen glove in tapestry weave. CENTRE Breast feather pattern in gold cloisonné with coloured glass inlay from the vulture collar on Tutankhamun's mummy. The colours are black, red (shown here as the dark screen) and pale green (light screen). BOTTOM The same pattern with different colour distribution on a miniature coffin. Tomb of Tutankhamun, Valley of the Kings. 18th Dynasty, New Kingdom (*c*. 1361–1352 BC). *Cairo Museum*. RIGHT Painted figure in wood. Height 1.12 m. Tomb of Meketre, Deir el-Bahri, no. 280, Thebes. 11th Dynasty, Middle Kingdom (*c*. 2000 BC). The pattern of her dress has been variously interpreted as embroidered cloth, leather appliqué or indeed as having been made with real feathers. *Metropolitan Museum of Art*, New York. (On dress see pp. 15–16, on cloisdonné p. 14).

64 The hassock is made of rushwork and lined with linen covered with beadwork. Tomb of Tutankhamun, Valley of the Kings. 18th Dynasty, New Kingdom (*c*. 1361–1352 BC). *Cairo Museum*.

65 LEFT TOP Painted design in black, blue and white on a red dress in the tomb of Queen Nefertari, no. 66, Thebes. 19th Dynasty, New Kingdom (*c*.

1304–1237 BC). BELOW examples of the bead design inlaid on various objects in Tutankhamun's tomb. From the top: on a breast ornament, the handle of the flabellum and a headrest. RIGHT Painted wooden figure of a servant from the tomb of Nakhti, Asyut. Middle Kingdom (*c*. 2040–1950 BC). *Cairo Museum*. (On cloisonne see p. 14, on dress see pp. 15–16.)

66 Painted ceiling patterns. TOP and CENTRE Tomb of Amenemhat, no. 48, Thebes. 18th Dynasty, New Kingdom (*c*. 1417–1379 BC). BOTTOM Tomb of Amenemhat, no. 82, Thebes. 18th Dynasty, New Kingdom (*c*. 1504–1450 BC). (On gridwork see note to 25, on painting p. 13.)

67 Painted ceiling patterns. TOP Tomb of Nebamun, no. 90, Thebes. 18th Dynasty, New Kingdom (*c*. 1425–1379 BC). CENTRE Drawing based on several examples of this 18th-dynasty design. BOTTOM Tomb of Kenamun, no. 162, Thebes. 18th Dynasty, New Kingdom (*c*. 1567–1320 BC). (On gridwork see note to 25, on painting p. 13, on the lily/palmette motif see pp. 19–20.)

68 LEFT The sash known as the 'Girdle of Ramesses III' is 5.2 m long and tapers from a width of 12.7 cm at one end to 4.8 cm at the other. It is in a double warp-face weave producing the same pattern on both faces. The plain middle section required four threads for each thread showing and the patterned borders on either side required five threads for each thread showing. As the sash tapers, groups of four warp threads were gradually taken out of the middle section until at the end only a thin white stripe remained. Groups of five threads from the patterned borders were taken out, gradually eliminating the narrower stripes, but leaving the main motif of the *ankh* sign and zig-zag intact to the end. The linen thread is 3-ply and the yarn about the thickness of fine sewing cotton. There are 1,689 warp threads and the count of threads showing on

the face is 68 × 30½ per inch. The predominant colour of the patterned borders is blue (medium screen) with some red (shown here as black, and a little yellow (light screen). (See M. Seagroatt, 'A Weaving Mystery: or New Light on an Old Girdle' and her references *Quarterly Journal of the Guild of Weavers Spinners and Dyers*, no. 50, June, 1964.) 20th Dynasty, New Kingdom (*c*. 1198–1166 BC). *Merseyside County Museums*, Liverpool. RIGHT This tapestry-woven textile was found in the tomb of Tuthmosis IV (no. 43, Valley of the Kings). The design, however, also includes the cartouche of his predecessor, Amenophis II (*c*. 1450–1425) and it may therefore have been an heirloom. The borders are attached by fine, black stitching which, in the case of the lotus border, became part of the design. The background colour is yellow, while the design is in black (shown here as black), red or brown (dark screen) and blue or green (light screen). Approximately actual size. *Cairo Museum*. (On weaving see pp. 16–17 and note to 70–71).

69 TOP Detail from wall painting in the tomb of Djehutyhefer, no. 104, Thebes. 18th Dynasty, New Kingdom (*c*. 1450–1425 BC). The painting is damaged and was originally rather sketchy. It has been slightly reconstructed with the aid of the original copier's notes in H. Ling Roth, *Ancient Egyptian and Greek Looms*, 2nd ed. 1951. BOTTOM Detail of wall painting in the tomb of Khnumhotpe no. 3, Beni Hasan. 12th Dynasty, Middle Kingdom (*c*. 1900 BC). (On weaving see pp. 15–16.)

70–71 The tunic was made from a length of fine linen folded in half; the selvages were sewn together at the sides leaving openings where the sleeves were attached. A hole and slit for the neck were cut in the front below the fold. There is a fringe at the lower edge. 113.5 × 95 cm. The condition of the embroidered panels, which make up some of the applied bands, is extremely

poor and little can be said about the original colours and techniques; only outline and chain stitch have been identified. The two panels reconstructed here (after W. Brunton in Crowfoot and Davies (see note to 61) shows the foreign—perhaps Syrian—character of the design. It is suggested that the panels, which alternate between figural and floral motifs, also had alternating dark and light backgrounds. Width 14 cm. The other bands which decorate the tunic (**71**) are in warp-face weave. To produce patterns of this kind two or more warp threads of different colours are threaded through each leash on the heddle rod and over the shed rod. The weaver choses the colour needed for the pattern and the other threads float at the back. The texture becomes very close and the pattern is in the warp with the weft entirely concealed. This technique could have been used on the ground loom illustrated **69** BOTTOM. This type of loom is similar to the Bedouin loom on which warp-face weave is produced today, albeit in coarse wool and with patterns in two colours only. Width of band CENTRE 14 cm. Tomb of Tutankhamun, Valley of the Kings. 18th Dynasty, New Kingdom (*c*. 1361–1352 BC). *Cairo Museum*. (On weaving and dress see pp. 15–16).

72 TOP Detail from wall painting in the tomb of Khnumhotpe, no. 3, Beni Hasan. 12th Dynasty, Middle Kingdom (*c*. 1900 BC). BOTTOM Details of patterns on a wall painting in the tomb of Menkheperresonb, no. 86, Thebes. 18th Dynasty, New Kingdom (*c*. 1504–1450 BC). (On dress see pp. 15–16.)

73 Figures made from thin wooden slats with heads in the round and hair of strung clay beads. LEFT Height 19 cm (6459), CENTRE height 26 cm (22631) *British Museum*. RIGHT Height 22 cm. *Cairo Museum*. 11th Dynasty, Middle Kingdom (*c*. 2040–2000 BC).

74 Painted ceiling patterns.

LEFT Tomb of Wahka II, Qaw el-Kebir. 12th Dynasty, Middle Kingdom (c. 1842–1797 BC). CENTRE tomb of Hepdjefa, Asyut. 12th Dynasty, Middle Kingdom (c. 1971–1928 BC). RIGHT Tomb of Amenemhat, no. 48, Thebes. 18th Dynasty, New Kingdom (c. 1417–1379 BC).

75 LEFT Painted ceiling pattern. Harem of Ramesses III, Medinet Habu. 20th Dynasty, New Kingdom (c. 1198–1166 BC) (After Prisse d'Avennes, see note to 44). The colours are green, blue and red on a black background. This painting has now disappeared. RIGHT Fragmentary carved wooden cosmetic spoon. Approx. actual size. (37924). 18th Dynasty, New Kingdom (c. 1400–1320 BC). *British Museum*.

76 Lidded cosmetic spoons carved in wood and inlaid with coloured paste: LEFT Height 14.3 cm. No provenance. CENTRE The lid is missing. Height 29.4 cm. ?Thebes. RIGHT Height 23.6 cm. Thebes. 18th–19th Dynasties (c. 1567–1200 BC). *Louvre*, Paris.

77 Cosmetic spoons carved in wood and inlaid with coloured paste: LEFT The lid is missing. Height 18 cm. No provenance. RIGHT This spoon had no lid. Height 22 cm. Gurna. *Louvre*, Paris. CENTRE The lid is missing. Height 21 cm. Sedment. *Petrie Museum, University College* (UC. 14365). London. 18th Dynasty, New Kingdom (c. 1400–1320 BC).

78 TOP Front and back view of a cosmetic spoon of carved wood. Length 18.5 cm. Medinet el-Ghorab (Faiyum). 18th Dynasty. BOTTOM Cosmetic spoon of blue glazed composition. Length 13.5 cm. 19th–20th Dynasties. New Kingdom (c. 1450–1085 BC). *Louvre*, Paris.

79 Cosmetic spoons of carved wood without lids. LEFT Height 26.5 cm. Gurna. *Cairo Museum*. CENTRE TOP Height 11.5 cm. Thebes. BOTTOM Height 13.3 cm. Thebes. RIGHT Height 19.5 cm. 18th Dynasty, New Kingdom (c. 1450–1320 BC). *Louvre*, Paris

80 TOP Front and back view of cosmetic spoon carved in ivory. Length 9 cm. No provenance. Middle Kingdom (c. 2000–1800 BC). CENTRE Cosmetic spoon carved in wood. Length 18.5 cm. 18th Dynasty, New Kingdom (c. 1450–1320 BC). *Louvre*, Paris. BOTTOM Cosmetic spoon carved in wood. Length 19.5 cm. (38187). 19th Dynasty, New Kingdom (c. 1250 BC). *British Museum*.

81 Cosmetic spoons carved in wood: TOP Length 27 cm. Memphis. (5945). CENTRE Length 18.5 cm. Thebes. (5952). 19th Dynasty, New Kingdom (c. 1300 BC). *British Museum*. BOTTOM Length 23.3 cm. Saqqara. 18th–19th Dynasties, New Kingdom (c. 1400–1200 BC) *Brooklyn Museum*, New York.

82 Designs painted in black on the inside of bowls in blue glazed composition ware. TOP Size not available. *Egyptian Museum*, Turin. 18th–19th Dynasty, New Kingdom (c. 1500–1200 BC). BOTTOM LEFT (22738) diameter 13.5 cm. 18th Dynasty, New Kingdom (c. 1450 BC). The painting on this bowl is rather shaky and has been tidied up a little in the drawing. RIGHT (30449) diameter 12 cm. Late New Kingdom (c. 1000 BC). *British Museum*. (On glazed composition see pp. 17–18.)

83 Designs painted in black on the inside of bowls in blue glazed composition ware. TOP diameter 20 cm. *Cairo Museum*. BOTTOM LEFT diameter 13.8 cm. Priv. coll. RIGHT diameter 10 cm. *Ägyptisches museum*, Berlin. 18th Dynasty, New Kingdom (c. 1450–1320 BC). (On glazed composition see pp. 17–18.)

84 Designs painted in black on the inside of bowls in blue glazed composition ware. TOP diameter 14 cm. New Kingdom (c. 1400–1085 BC). BOTTOM LEFT (35120) diameter 10.4 cm; RIGHT (48657) diameter 12 cm. Late New Kingdom (c. 1000 BC). *British Museum*. (On glazed composition see pp. 17–18.)

85 Designs painted in black on the inside of bowls in blue glazed composition ware. TOP

(4790) diameter 25 cm. Thebes. 18th Dynasty, New Kingdom (c. 1450 BC) BOTTOM LEFT (13153) diameter 14 cm. Faiyum; RIGHT (36409) diameter 11 cm (reconstructed) Late New Kingdom (c. 1000 BC). *British Museum*. (On glazed composition see pp. 17–18.)

86 Mirrors of bronze. TOP (37173) length 23.5 cm. BOTTOM LEFT (32583) length 19 cm. *British Museum*. RIGHT length 25.4 cm. *Berlin Museum*. 18th Dynasty, New Kingdom (c. 1567–1400 BC).

87 TOP (57900) length 11.2 cm, Abydos. New Kingdom (c. 1300 BC). BOTTOM RIGHT (2736) length 23.6 cm. Thebes. Middle Kingdom (c. 1900 BC). *British Museum*. BOTTOM LEFT length 26.5 cm. *Petrie Museum, University College* (no reg. number). London.

88–89 Early seals of various shapes. The *British Museum* registration numbers are listed below: 88 TOP LEFT (67349), TOP CENTRE (28734), TOP RIGHT (40763), CENTRE (64987), BOTTOM LEFT (64857), BOTTOM RIGHT (48993). 89 From left to right: TOP (42994) (32361) (no number), BOTTOM (40761) (64859) (3852). (On seals see p. 18.)

90 From left to right: TOP *Scarabaeus sacer* L., Both sides of a scarab amulet with a loop on the underside (3483); CENTRE (37711) (39198); BOTTOM (27194) (53721) *British Museum*. (On seals see p. 18.)

91–100 Scarab seal designs. Many different materials were used to make scarabs, the most common are steatite and glazed composition, but ivory, bone and semi-precious stones also occur. No dates are indicated for the scarab seal designs; most were produced over very long periods. The *British Museum* registration numbers are listed below.

91 From left to right: TOP (63149) above (53483) below (58596) (53671), CENTRE (62483) (65810) (58561), BOTTOM (46596) (62434) (58346) (3869).

92 From left to right: TOP (27013) (66740) (39946), CENTRE

(39440) (39613) (46687), BOTTOM (54683) (49974) (53235).

93 From left to right: TOP (50007) (43086) (65384), small designs below (17532) (51278), CENTRE (42555) (54442) (42946), BOTTOM (27194) (27947) (27947) (48851) (39620).

94 From left to right: TOP (42659) (45429) (40467), CENTRE (42773) (49968), BOTTOM (48717) (53730) (52068).

95 From left to right: TOP (50008) (45789) (45480), CENTRE (39067) (33911) (66757), BOTTOM (42955) (49993) (28533).

96 From left to right: TOP (39096) (39680) (27822), CENTRE (45627) (45614) (41947), BOTTOM (41904) (45801) (42232).

97 From left to right: TOP (48944) (52997) (28175), CENTRE (28108) (52023) (3864) (39392), BOTTOM (40294) (27872) (46945) (39439).

98 From top to bottom: LEFT (17547) (28852) (51977), CENTRE (42415) (52260) (17515) (51318) (27772), RIGHT (27221) (3833) (45931).

99 From top to bottom: LEFT (59008) (17500) (82186) (27106), CENTRE (58157) (53674) (38913), RIGHT (57109) (3681) (26605) (53721).

100 From left to right: TOP (39100) (46822) (39068), CENTRE (57054) (17395) (30684) (53490), BOTTOM (41941) (40274) (39413) (47206). (On seals see p. 18.)

Further reading

ALDRED C.
Jewels of the Pharaohs
London 1971

ALDRED C.
Egyptian Art,
London 1985

BIERBRIER M.
The Tomb-Builders of the Pharaohs,
London 1982

EDWARDS I. E. S.
Tutankhamen, his tomb and its treasures,
London 1979

GOMBRICH E. H.
The Sense of Order. A Study in the Psychology of Decorative Art,
London 1979

JAMES T. G. H.
An Introduction to Ancient Egypt,
London 1979

JAMES T. G. H.
Egyptian Paintings,
London 1985

PECK W. H.
Drawings from Ancient Egypt,
London 1978

SMITH W. S.
*The Art and Architecture of
Ancient Egypt,*
Harmondsworth 1958

The Designs

1 Hippopotamus in water, painted in white on a burnished red background inside a predynastic bowl from the 4th millennium BC.

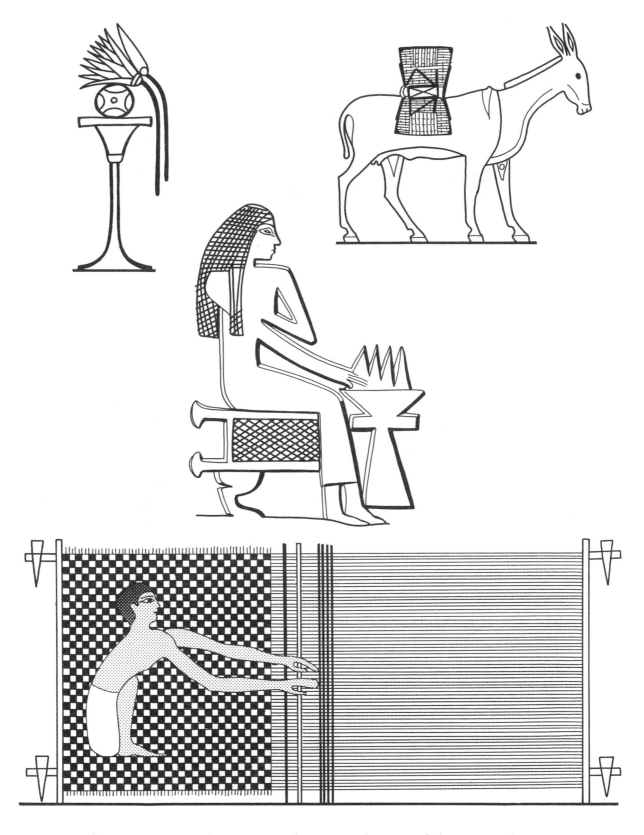

2 The Egyptians sought to express the essential nature of objects, not the impressions of a moment or a view from a particular angle. Several views were therefore combined to make up the one image: the bread lies on the table, the donkey has panniers on both sides, the woman sits on the seat and the weaver works at a horizontal ground loom.

3 Offerings, painted on the wall of a tomb, depict produce spread out on the ground. The nearest objects are shown at the bottom while those further away are placed higher up. The conventions of aspective representation were established at the beginning of the 3rd millennium BC and remained largely unchanged for nearly three thousand years.

4 Egyptian art is essentially two-dimensional; there is no attempt to create the illusion of space in this representation of a man kneeling by a pond in the shade of a doum palm.

5 TOP LEFT Three different drawings of the same subject – a jug standing in a basin – all allow the shapes of both vessels to be seen clearly. BOTTOM The garden pool surrounded by trees is a perfect and satisfactory example of the Egyptian aspective convention.

6 Another characteristic of Egyptian art is its apparent realism achieved by conventional images. Despite the convincingly natural appearance of the flock of birds from a tomb-painting TOP, all the birds have the same conventionalized body with wings attached to its outline in different positions, as shown BOTTOM.

7 Many common motifs were strictly conventionalized: the poppy, cornflower and mandrake fruit are here seen in different contexts, TOP and CENTRE painted in a more or less naturalistic style, BOTTOM inlaid on a piece of furniture. The form of the flowers and fruit varies little and reappears in these forms on many occasions in this book.

8 Predynastic bowls are decorated internally with painted designs in white or cream on a burnished red background. Mid-4th millennium BC.

9 The internal designs on these bowls, and on those OPPOSITE, occur in basketry and weaving – crafts also known from this early period. These media may be a source for such patterns. The designs BOTTOM deviate from the strictly repetitive formulae of the others. Mid-4th millennium BC.

10 The ornament on these predynastic pots are early examples of the tendency in Egyptian art to avoid strict and mechanical repetition and to introduce motifs taken from nature. Mid-4th millennium BC.

11 The pottery is hand raised, well made with thin walls. Shapes are simple and usually without handles or rims. Mid-4th millennium BC.

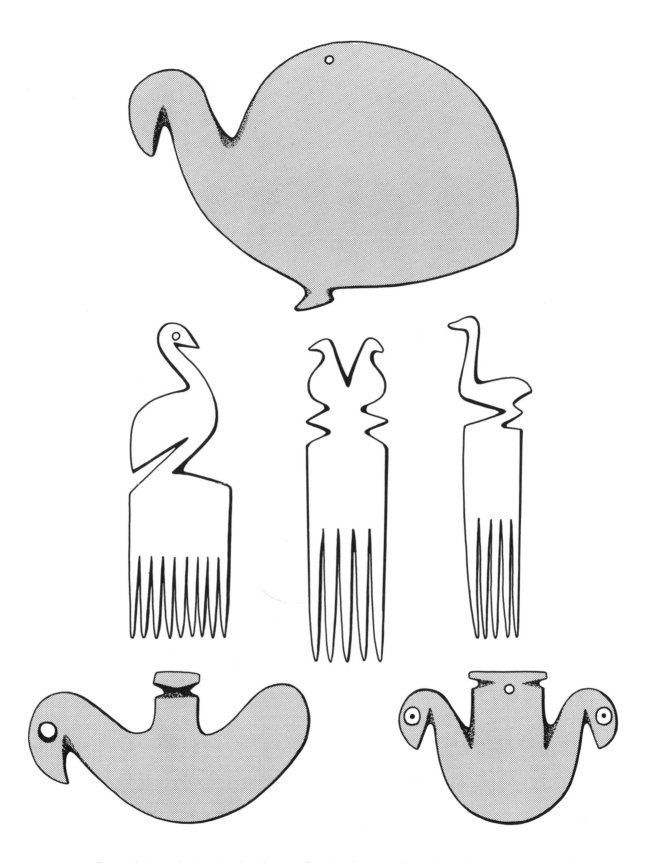

12 Grey slate palettes in the form of animals are often found in the graves of
the Predynastic Period. In many instances the eyes are inlaid with white shell.
Combs of ivory from the tusks of hippopotamuses and elephants are also often
carved in animal form. 4th millennium BC.

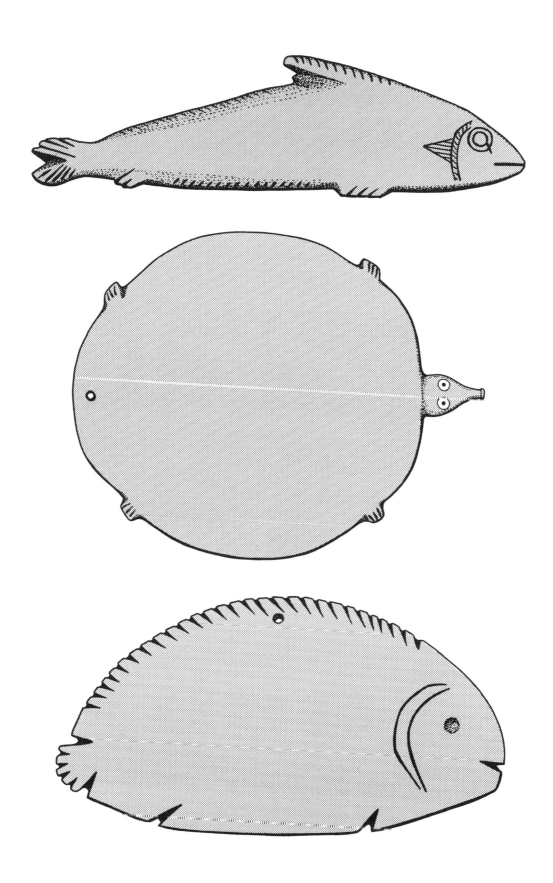

13 It is thought that palettes were used to grind and mix the colours used for eye make-up.

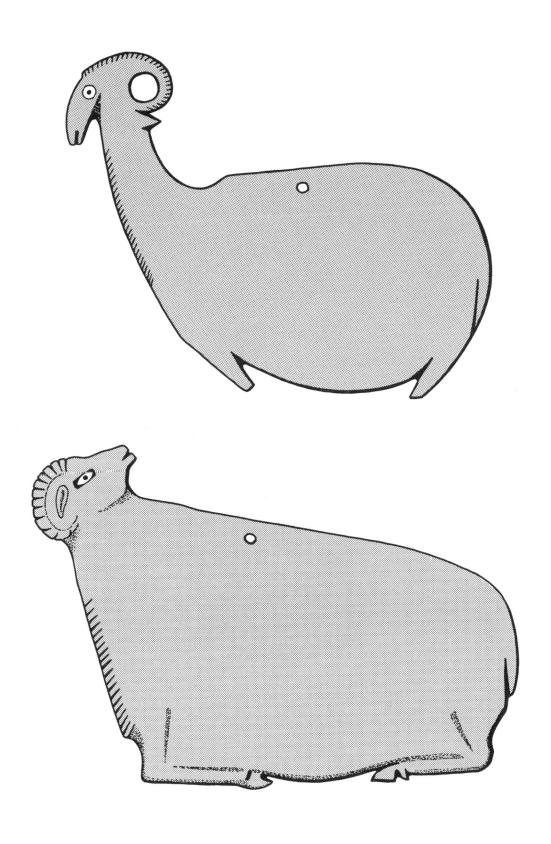

14 Predynastic slate palettes.

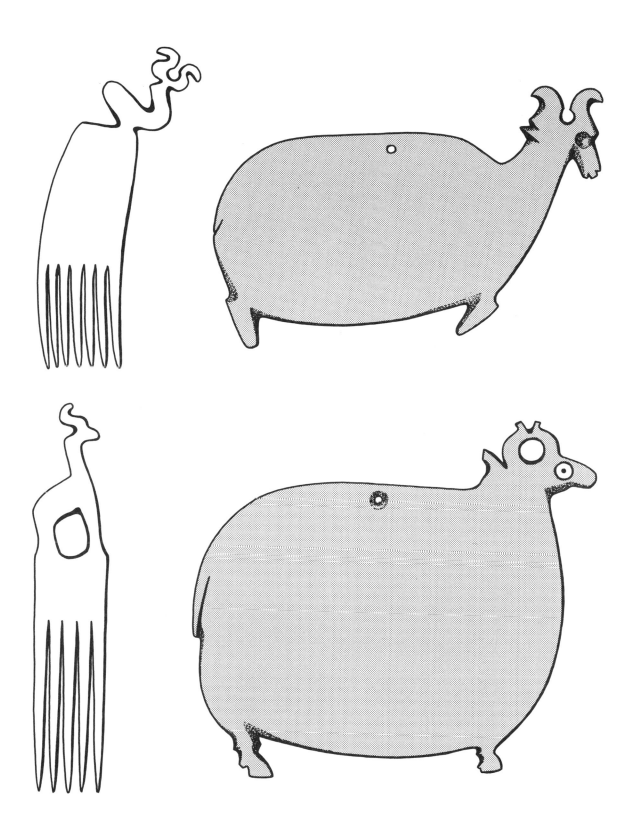

15 Predynastic slate palettes and combs. 4th millennium BC.

16 A different, and later, type of predynastic pottery has painted designs in red on a buff background. The motifs typically reflect a marshy river environment with birds and a mysterious plant, tentatively identified as the Abyssinian banana tree, drawn here for comparison after an 18th-century print. Late 4th millennium BC.

17 Among the natural features, like the jumping antelopes, are those which suggest religious ritual. This seems the most likely interpretation of the boat with many oars and the dancing women. Late 4th millennium BC.

18 Basketry is one of the oldest crafts known. In Egypt baskets are often shown, filled with produce, in wall-paintings. These examples are from an Old Kingdom tomb-painting. *c.* 2400 BC.

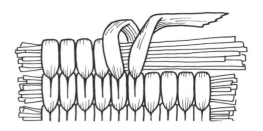
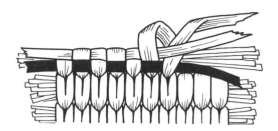

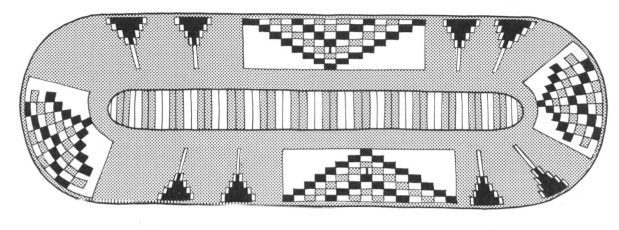

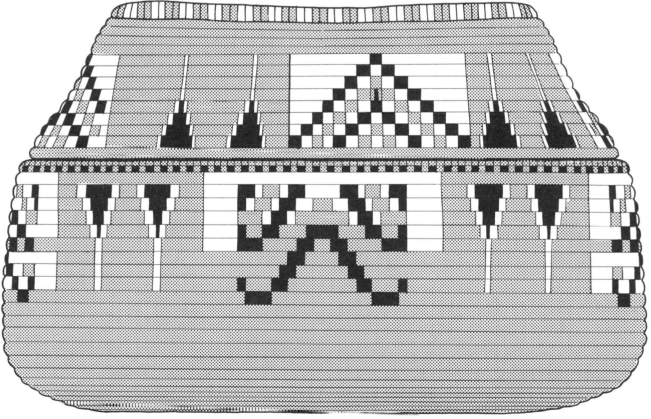

19 Most Egyptian baskets were made by the coiled method. The diagram TOP LEFT shows the split stitch used in the making of the lidded oval basket depicted below. The method used to finish off and strengthen the edge is shown TOP RIGHT.

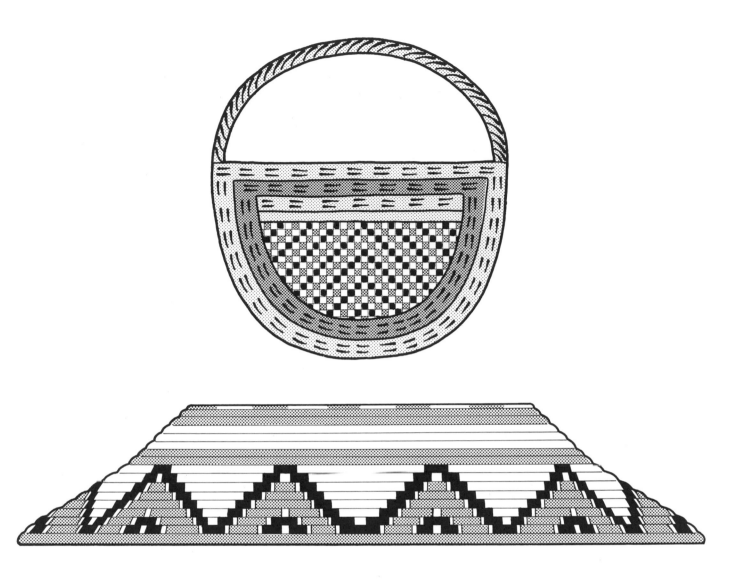

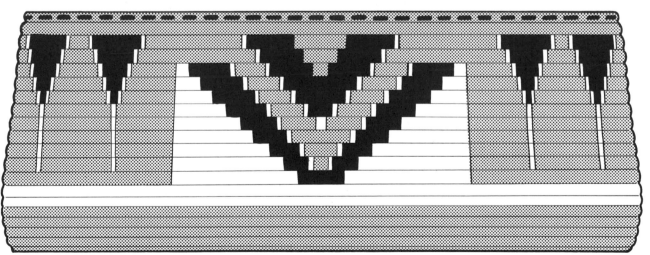

20 TOP Basket with handle as painted on a coffin. BELOW Oval lid and oval basket executed in the coiled method. The colour is reddish brown with the design in black and buff.

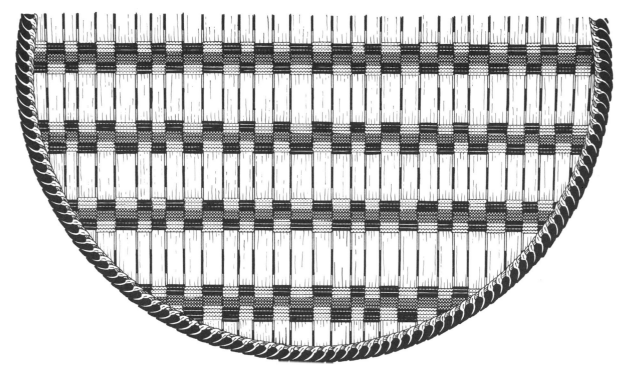

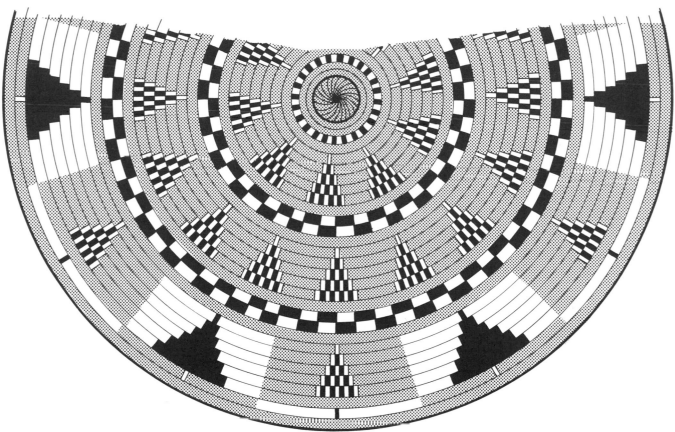

21 TOP Detail of circular mat made up of two layers of slats bound together by rows of red, green and buff fibre in twined weaving. There are two rows of sewing round the edge. BELOW Detail of slightly conical, circular basket lid in coiled technique.

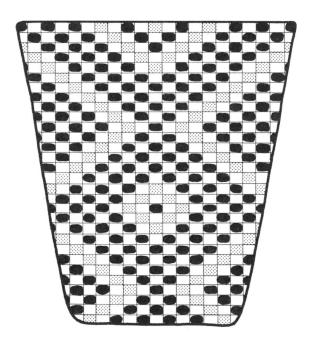
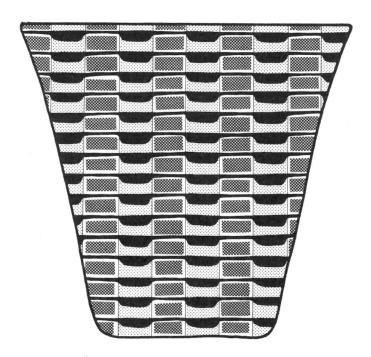

22 Wall-paintings in tombs of the New Kingdom demonstrate the rich variety of patterns which could be achieved in basketry.

23 In these paintings of baskets there is no attempt to suggest a rounded shape by the foreshortening of patterns to the sides. Such means were never used in Egyptian art to create the illusion of space.

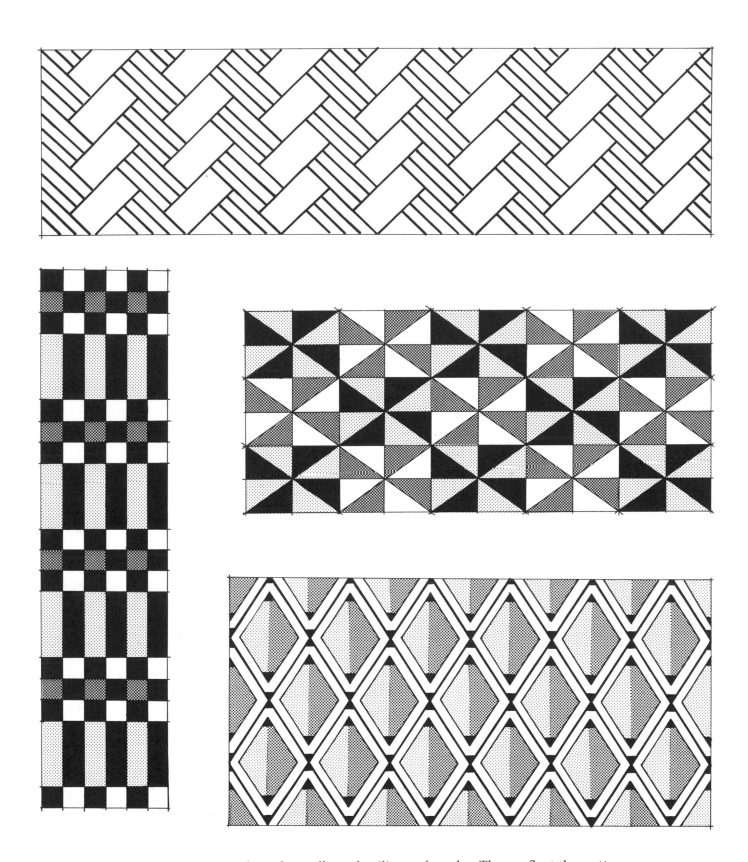

24 Designs painted on the walls and ceilings of tombs. They reflect the patterns of woven matting originally used to line the tombs. The design TOP is from the beginning of the 2nd millennium BC and the remainder from the beginning of the 3rd millennium BC.

25 Painted ceiling patterns. The interlocking character of these patterns is thought to reflect influences from the Minoan culture in the Aegean, an area in which Egypt had trade contacts during the Middle Kingdom at the beginning of the 2nd millennium BC. The gridwork is not original.

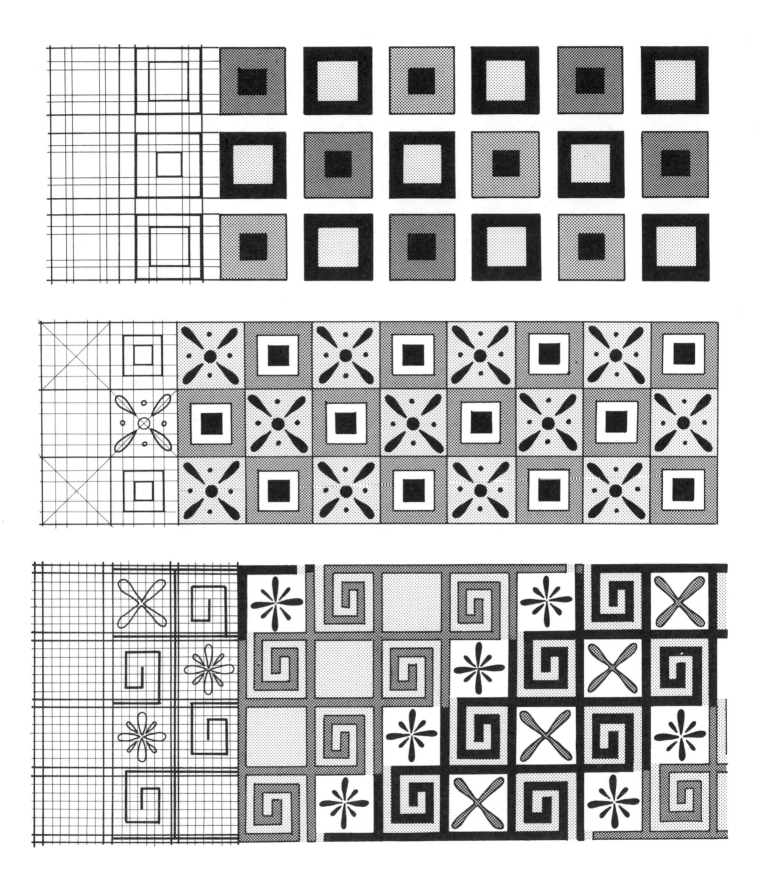

26 Painted ceiling patterns. These simple motifs remain in use throughout the whole of the Dynastic Period alongside more intricate designs. The gridwork is not original.

27 The use of colour is important in the ceiling patterns. Variation is achieved in these simple patterns by alternating the basic range of colours: blue, red, yellow, green, black and white (indicated here by screens of different density). The gridwork is not original.

28 The papyrus, LEFT, can reach a height of 5 m; it has a leafless stem of triangular cross-section, with leaf-sheaths at the base, and flowers carried on long fronds in a large umbel at the top. It is one of the most important motifs in Egyptian art. Some of the conventional forms of the motif are shown RIGHT.

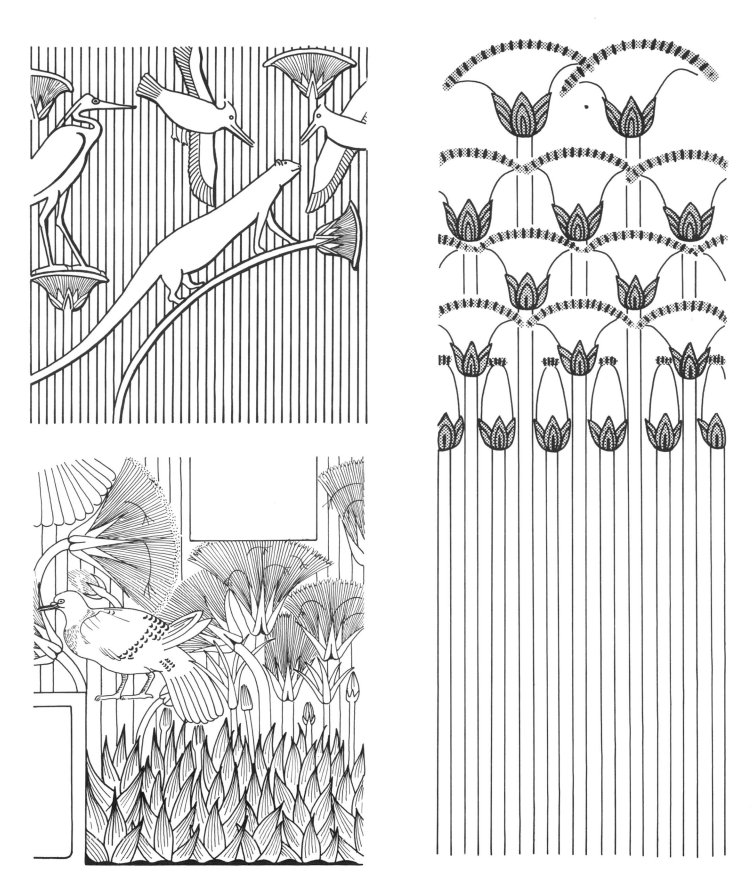

29 The groves of tall papyrus are often the background to hunting scenes in wall-paintings, represented in a highly conventionalized form: TOP from the Old Kingdom, RIGHT from the New Kingdom and BOTTOM in a more naturalistic treatment from the Amarna period, when the conventional forms were briefly relaxed.

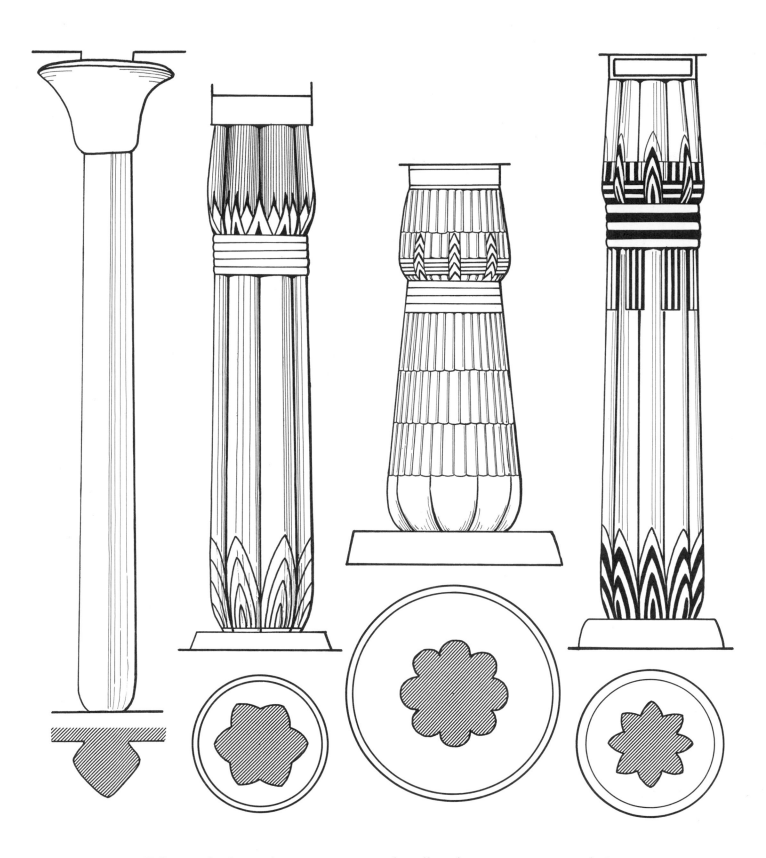

30 Pillars in the form of papyrus stems, or bundles of papyrus, were translations in stone for tombs and temples of the light materials used in domestic house construction.

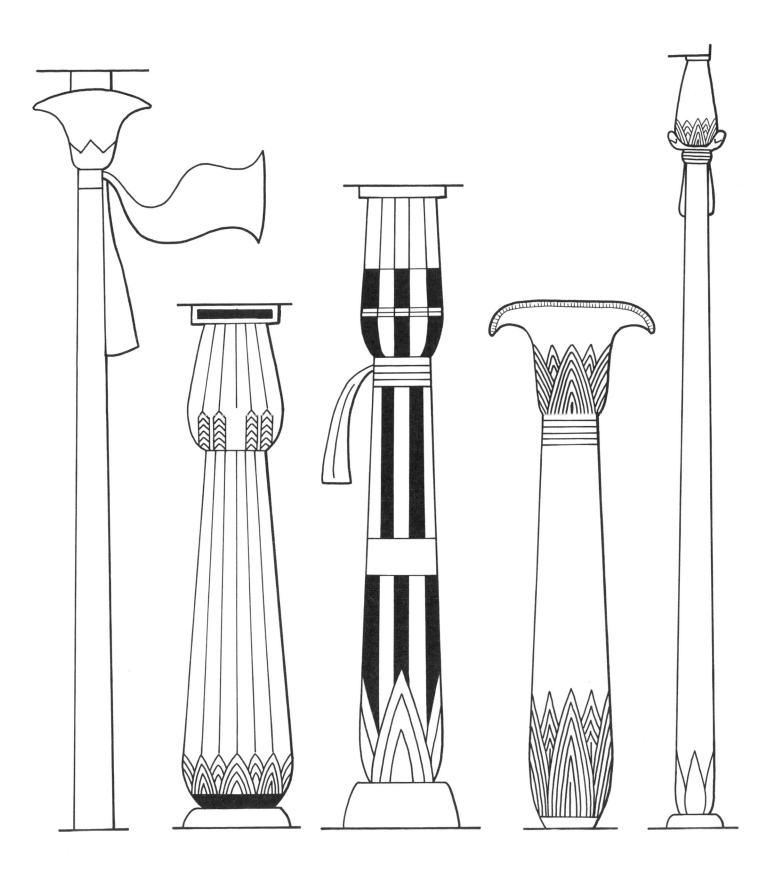

31 Tomb-paintings often include representations of architectural detail. The papyrus pillar is distinguished by the short outer leaves of the umbel – which may be either open or in bud, and the swelling towards the base of the stem surrounded by leaf-sheaths.

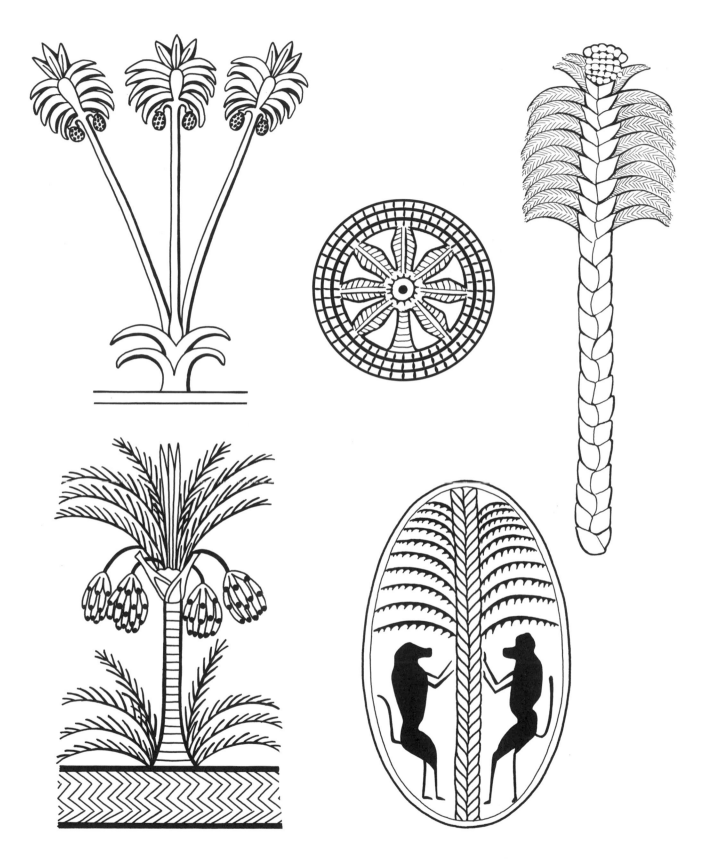

32 The date palm was a very important tree in Egypt; it was cultivated and all its parts provided essential material and food. From the earliest times it was a popular motif in art. Carved, painted and moulded examples are shown here.

33 The slender wooden pillar LEFT is an early example of the palm motif used
for this purpose. In stone it produced one of the most impresssive features
of Egyptian architecture.

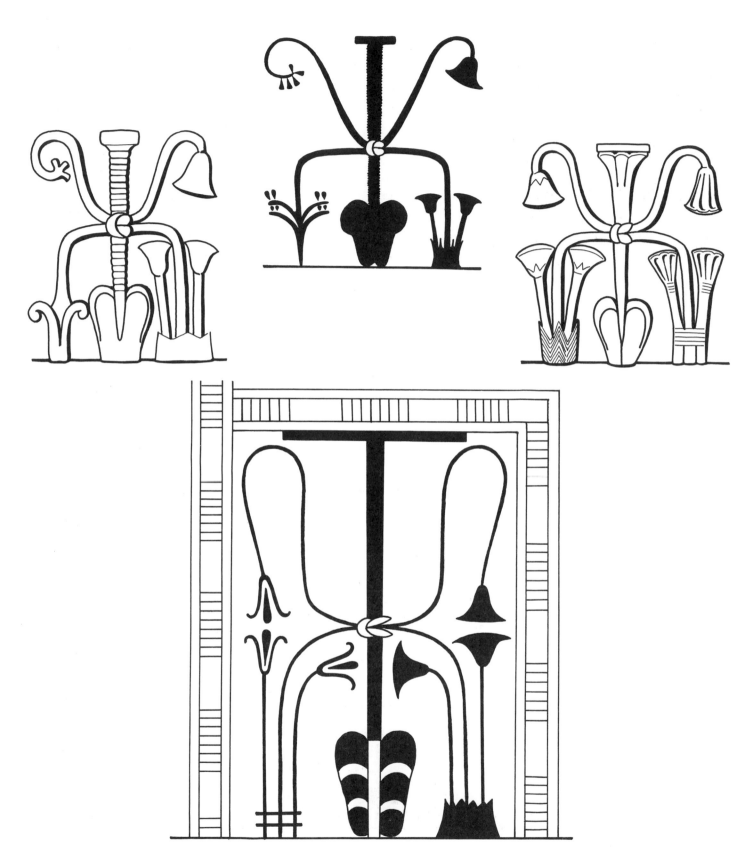

34 The sign which symbolizes the Unification of Upper and Lower Egypt, the South, or Upper Egypt, is represented in earlier versions by a sedge-like plant, or even a palm, TOP later it becomes the flower motif known as the 'Lily of the South'. BOTTOM The North, or Lower Egypt, is represented by the papyrus.

35 The sign which stands between the heraldic plants is the lung-and-trachea hieroglyph which means 'to unite'. The close interdependence between hieroglyphic writing and representational drawing is illustrated TOP where two figures are shown knotting the stems of the plants together round the sign.

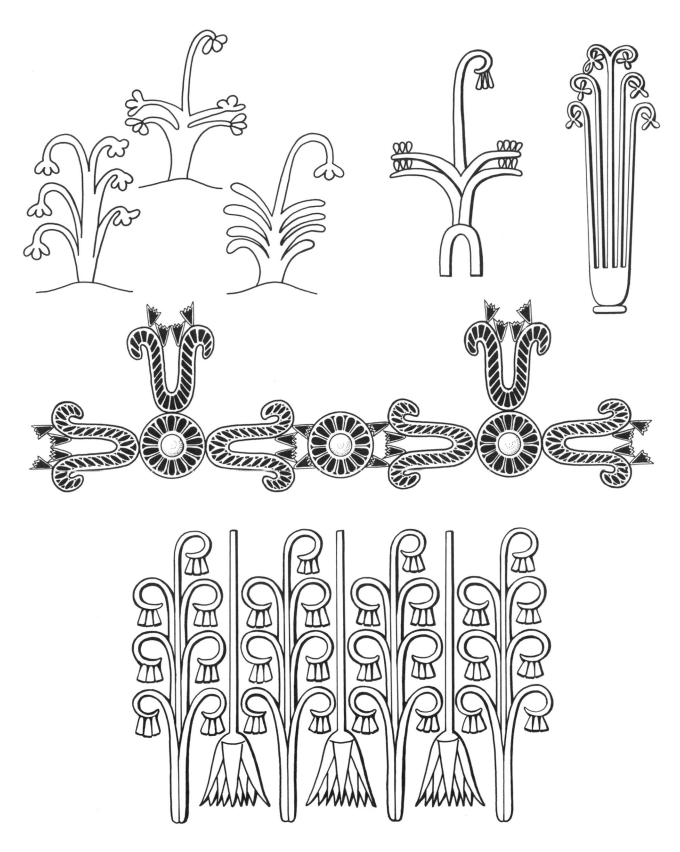

36 Drawings of flowering sedge-like plants and the stylized hieroglyphic sign for the South, TOP second from RIGHT, as well as other designs made up of curved plant elements, may have contributed to the development of the lily motif. There is no actual plant which can convincingly be identified as its model.

37 *Chrysanthemum coronarium* L. TOP LEFT was obviously the inspiration for the ivory box TOP RIGHT and perhaps also for other simple rosette motifs. More complex rosettes appear to have been inspired by a variety of plant elements, BOTTOM.

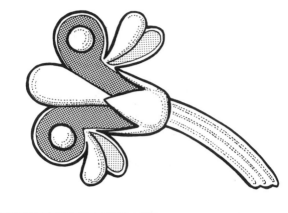

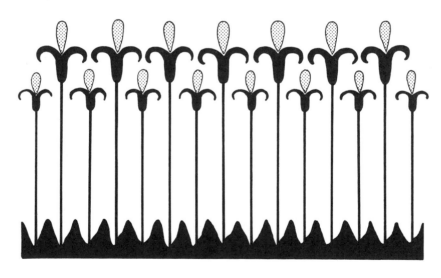

38 In the tomb of Tutankhamun are many objects decorated with the lily motif: TOP and CENTRE in gold cloisonné inlaid with stones in red (shown here as black), blue (dark screen) and green (light screen). The design BOTTOM is painted black and red. *c.* 1361 – 1352 BC.

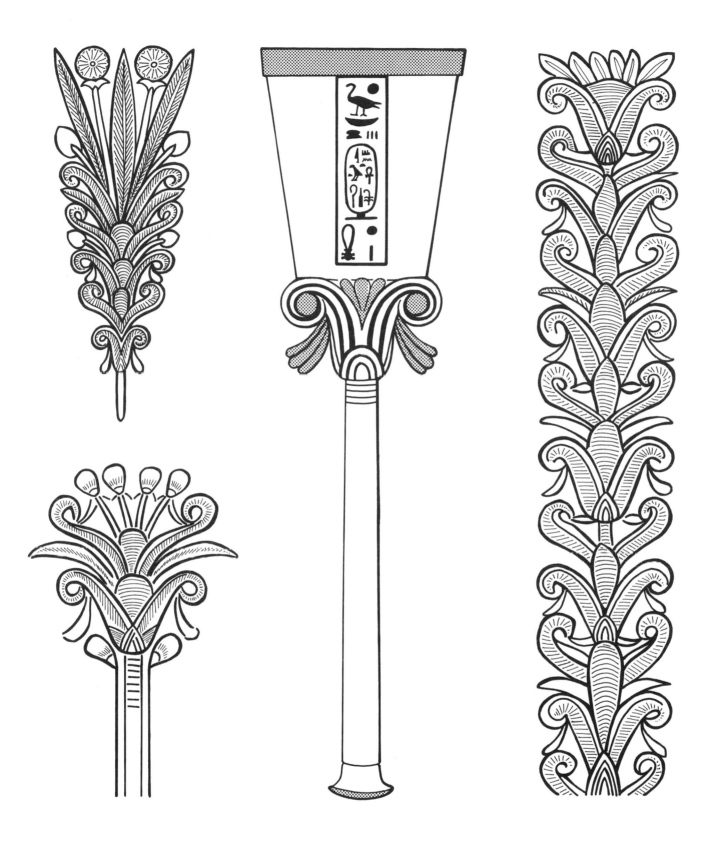

39 Other objects in Tutankhamun's tomb are decorated with more elaborate variations on the lily motif in palmette-like designs. The inscription on the ivory 'papyrus burnisher' CENTRE reads: Son of Re, Lord of Appearances – Tutankhamun Ruler of Southern Heliopolis – like Re. *c.* 1361 – 1352 BC.

40 The lotus motif is the most common in Egyptian art; it was based on two distinctive species of water-lilies, the white and the blue lotus. The white lotus LEFT is distinguished by the rounded shape of the flower, the pronounced ribs on the calyx leaves and the scalloped edge of the round leaf.

41 White lotus flowers are attached to a headdress in a tomb-painting TOP LEFT. The motif is typically used on rounded bowls and chalices, as in the examples OPPOSITE, and particularly well in the magnificent alabaster lamp in Tutankhamun's tomb BOTTOM.

42 The blue lotus LEFT is the commonest motif of all. The flower is distinguished by its triangular, pointed shape, the spotted calyx leaves and the smooth edge of the leaf. In the conventional form of the motif, the spots on the calyx leaves are not always represented and the water-lily character is ignored, as in the design RIGHT CENTRE.

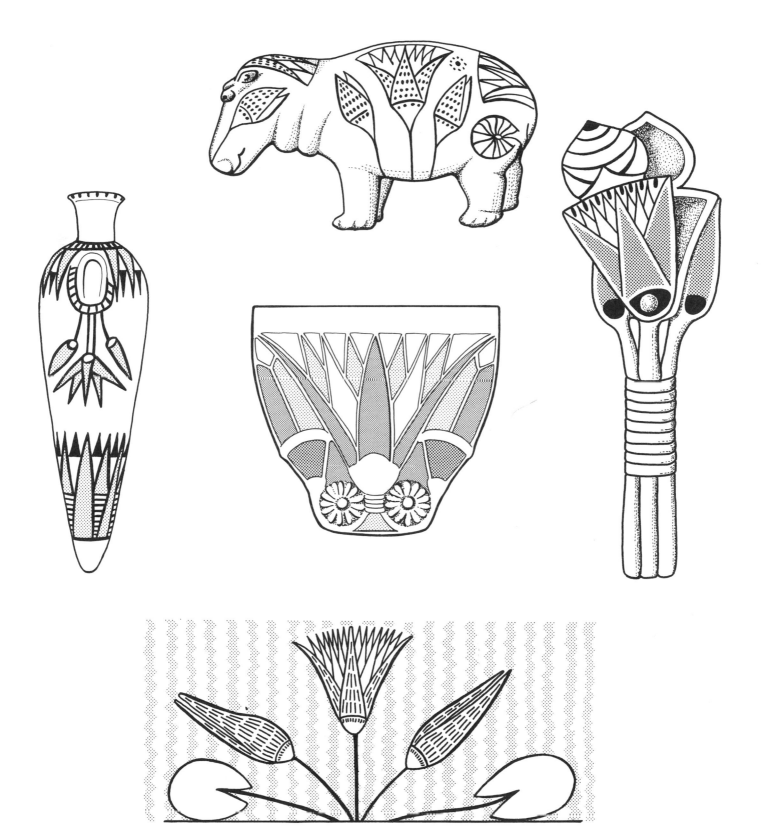

43 The lotus flower with a bud on either side is a constant motif which is used in every kind of material and technique. These examples are in painting, carved wood, glazed composition and gold cloisonné.

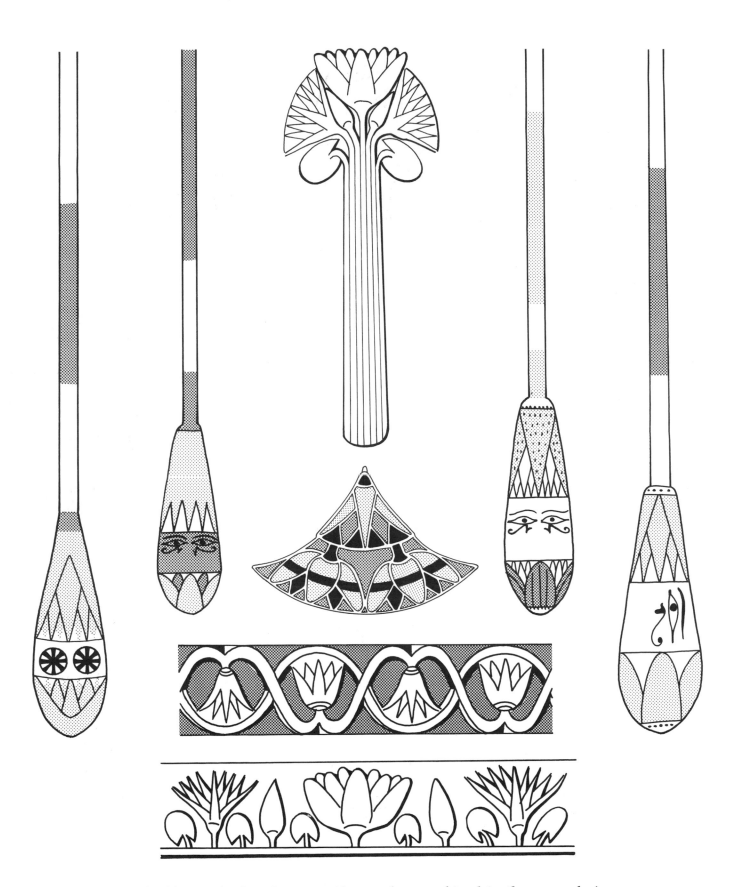

44 The blue and white lotus motifs are often combined in the same design. On the blades of these oars, from model boats, for instance, they decorate the pointed and the rounded ends respectively.

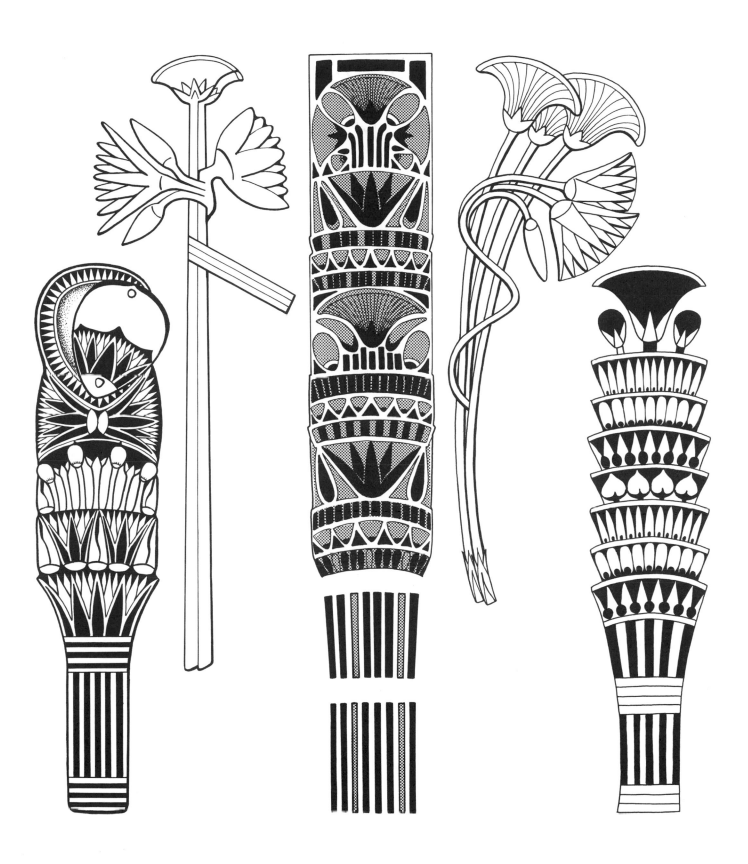

45 The staff of papyrus wound round with blue and white lotus flowers SECOND from LEFT perfectly illustrates the differences between these three major motifs in Egyptian art. Tall flower arrangements are commonly-used decorative devices.

46 Garlands of flowers and petals are found with some mummies. TOP shows
a reconstruction of two strands of a garland made from lotus petals and leaves.
Garlands became a popular decorative theme as collars and borders.

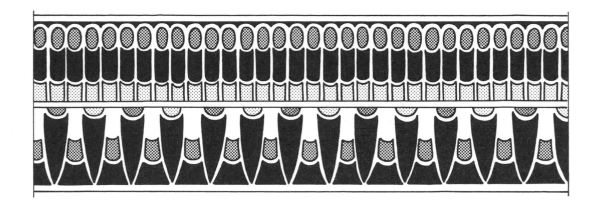

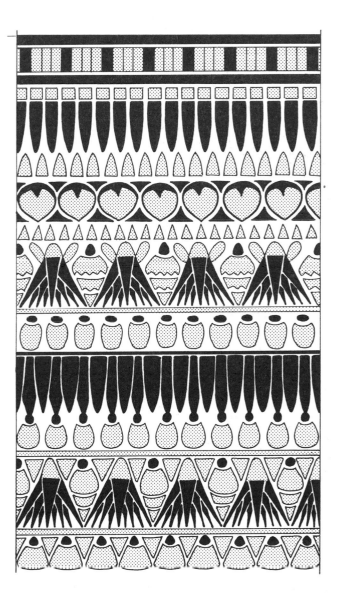

47 Apart from lotus flowers and petals, mandrake fruit, cornflowers, poppy petals etc. can be distinguished in these decorative designs produced in a variety of techniques.

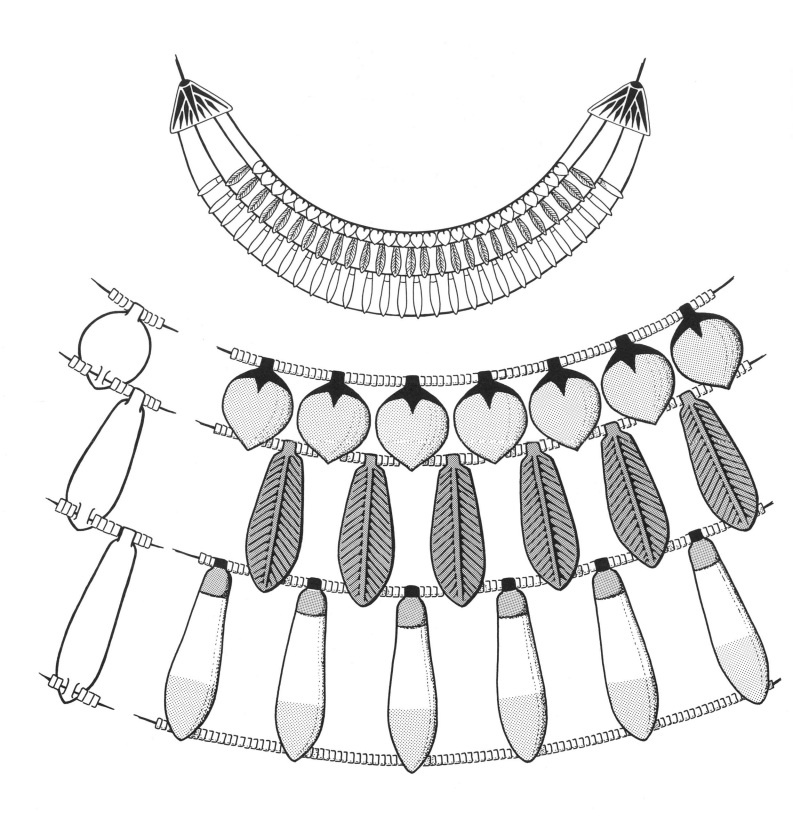

48 TOP Collar of glazed beads. Each bead is strung on two strands – top and bottom – and is separated by small spacer beads. The strands are held by terminals which have four holes at the bottom and a single hole at the top. Details of the stringing are shown BOTTOM. Scale approx. 3:2. *c.* 1379 – 1362 BC.

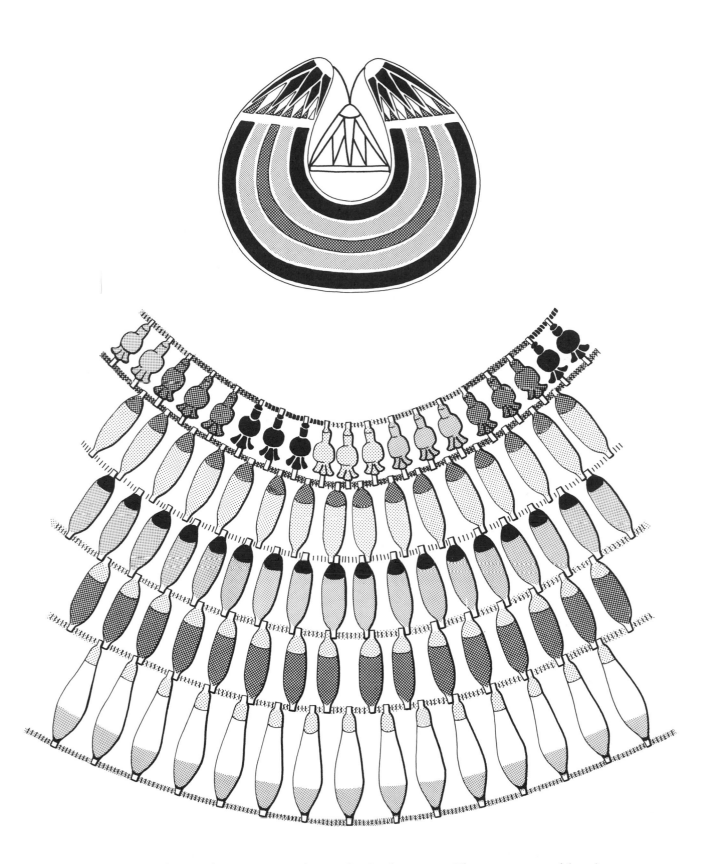

49 TOP Collar with a counterpoise at the back. BELOW The sequence of beads in a collar: cornflowers in alternate groups of blue, yellow, green and red; three rows of figs, yellow with red tops, green with blue tops and red with yellow tops. The last row is of white lotus petals with yellow tops and pale blue tips. Scale approx. 3:2.

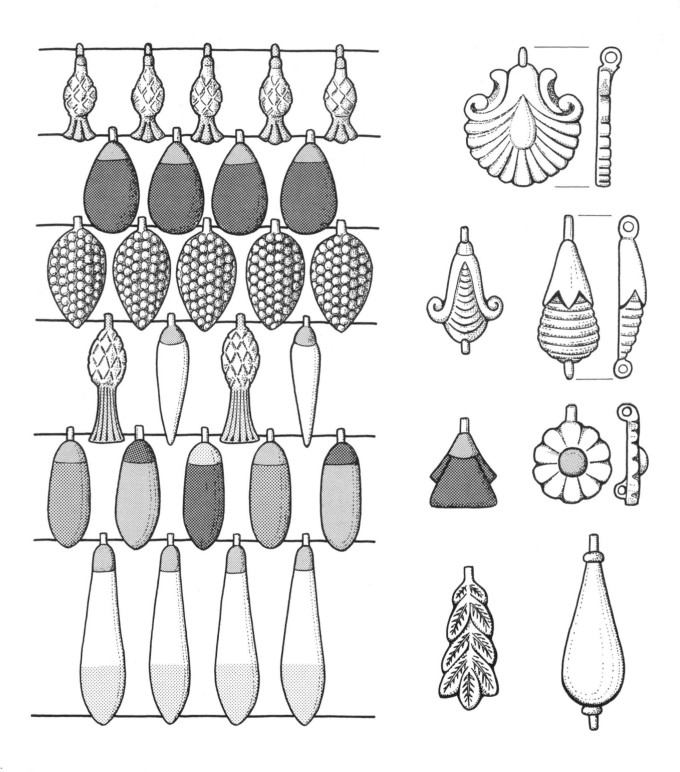

50 LEFT Sequence of glazed beads which made up a collar on seven strands. The shapes include blue and green cornflowers, red poppy petals, blue bunches of grapes, figs of different colours and lotus petals. Other bead-shapes are shown RIGHT and BOTTOM OPPOSITE. Scale approx. 3:2.

51 TOP Necklace of carnelian and gold beads with cloisonné pendants in the shape of mandrake fruit. The pendant CENTRE LEFT is of gold inlaid with the design of a petal collar in carnelian, lapis lazuli and turquoise, while the small animal pendants and ornaments are of gold.

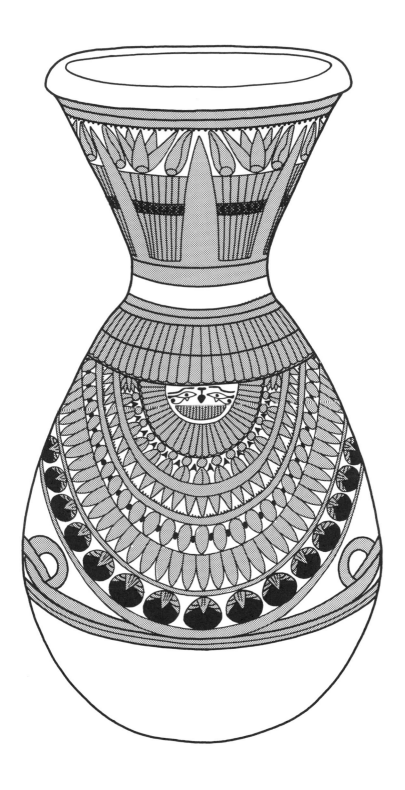

52 Pottery was not decorated in Egypt after the Predynastic Period, except during a brief interlude in the 18th Dynasty of the New Kingdom; the large wine jar from El-Amarna is typical of this ware. The ornament of garlands and flowers is painted in light blue on a cream slip with minor details in black and red.

53 LEFT Petals and the blue-lotus-and-bud motifs decorate this jar. The detail from a tomb-painting RIGHT also demonstrates the preference for these motifs in the pottery of this type.

54 The lotus motifs were also applied to pillars. Pillars with a single shaft are shown on many wall-paintings and probably represent light wooden structures, while in stone, bundles of stems are usually represented. The capitals of these examples appear to show the more rounded shape of the white lotus.

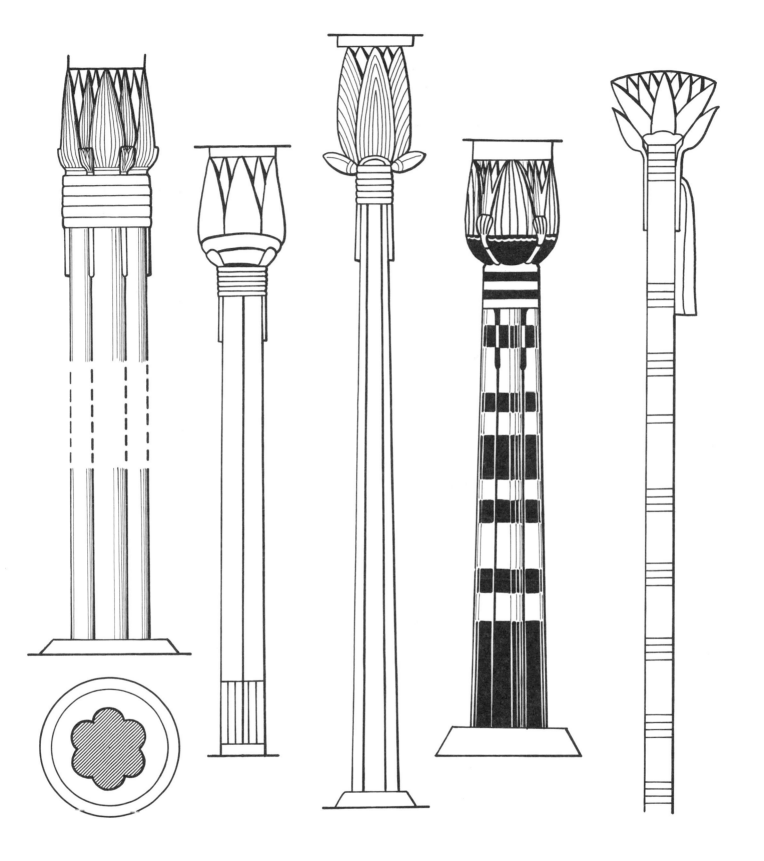

55 Lotus pillars can be distinguished by their straight shafts and by the equal length of both petals and calyx leaves. The capitals of these examples suggest the shape of the blue lotus.

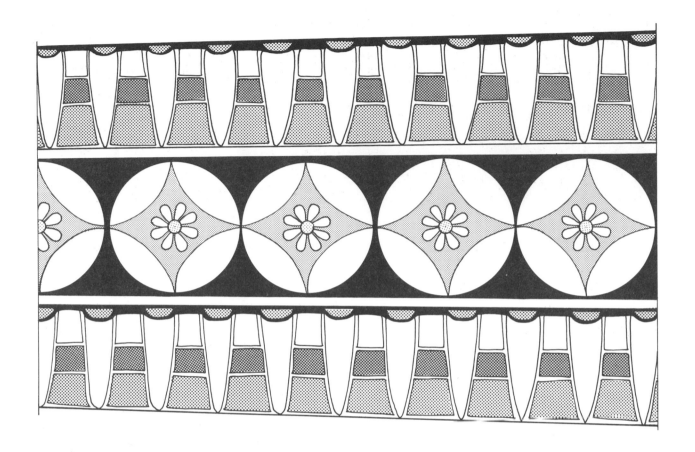

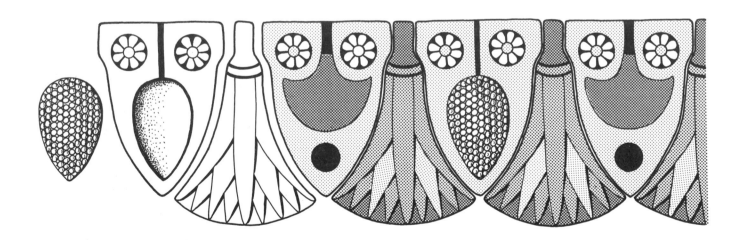

56 Plant motifs also decorate other architectural features like borders and friezes in mosaic. The individual elements of stone or glazed composition were produced separately and were set in a matrix, which was sometimes coloured and left exposed to contribute to the design.

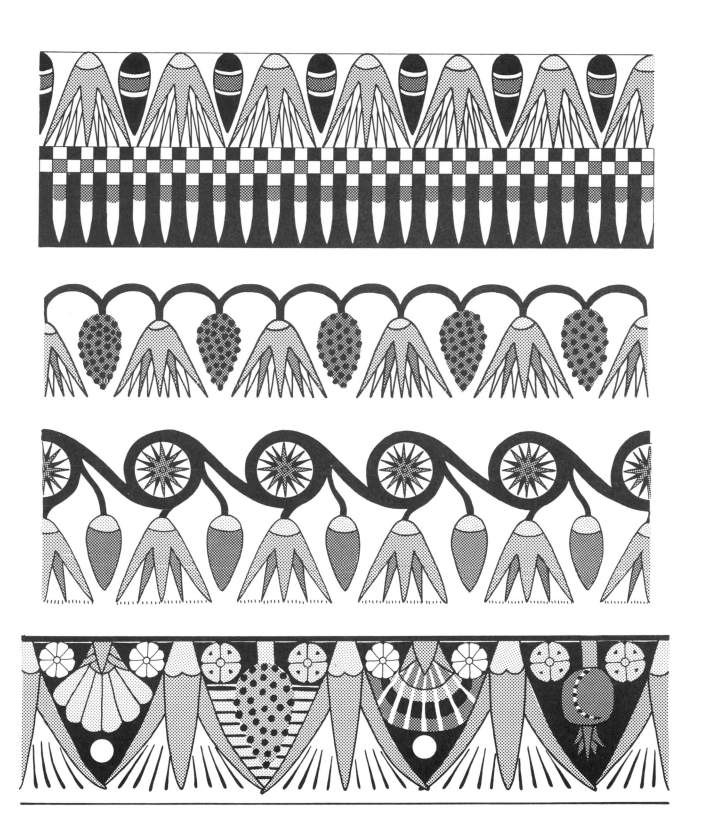

57 In the tomb-paintings, friezes and borders are often part of the design – some examples are shown here.

58 Ceiling patterns with scroll designs often incorporate plant motifs in simple repetitive patterns. The gridwork is not original.

59 The intricate construction of these ceiling patterns is most unusual in Egyptian art. They are among the latest designs illustrated in this book. 7th century BC. The gridwork is not original.

60 The sun-god Re-Harakhty is splendidly portrayed as a hawk in this breast ornament in gold cloisonné inlaid with blue glass (here shown as black), red carnelian (dark screen) and turquoise (light screen). The breast, wing and tail feather patterns are common motifs in Egyptian art. From the tomb of Tutankhamun, *c.* 1361 – 1352 BC.

61 The stylized wing feather pattern has been translated LEFT into a woven design on a band in warp-face weave (the arrow indicates the direction of the warp) and RIGHT into a repeat pattern in gold cloisonné. CENTRE An ostrich feather fan depicted in carved and gilded wood. From the tomb of Tutankhamun, *c.* 1361 – 1352 BC.

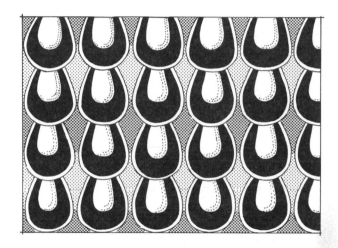
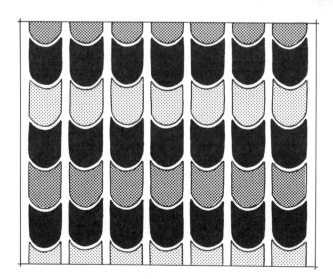

62 The examples of feather patterns in embossed and chased gold and cloisonné on this page and OPPOSITE LEFT are from objects in Tutankhamun's tomb and demonstrate some variations on this motif. *c.* 1361 – 1352 BC.

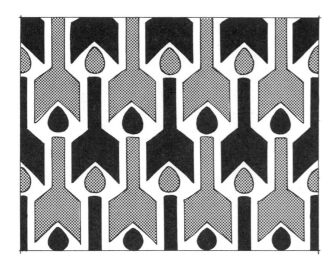

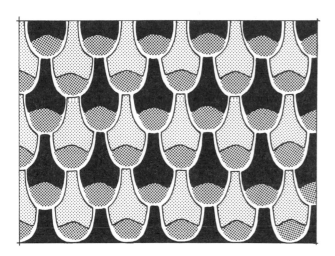

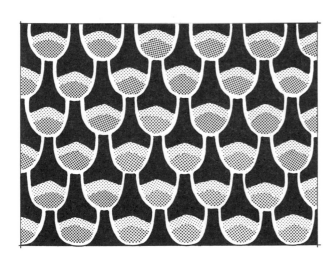

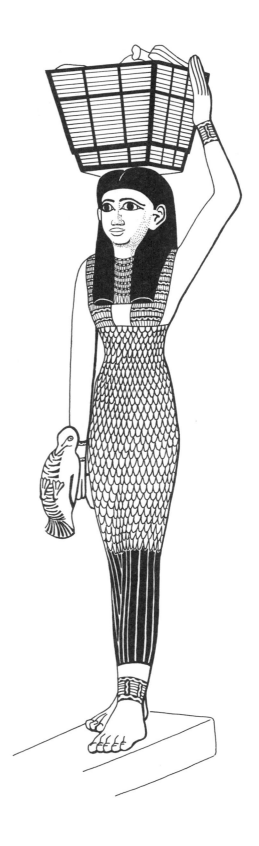

63 The design TOP LEFT is from a glove in tapestry weave from Tutankhamun's tomb. The actual dress, copied on the figure of the girl RIGHT, may have been made of real feathers.

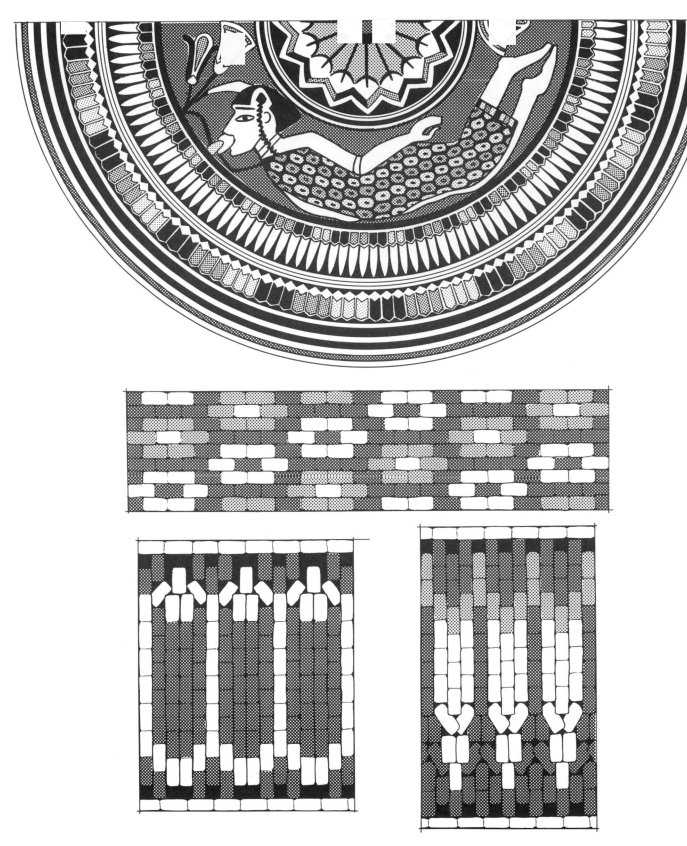

64 TOP Part of the design of a hassock in beadwork from Tutankhamun's tomb. It depicts a bound and gagged prisoner in a flowered dress, floating among water plants. The hassock is bordered by petal and feather patterns. An attempt to show how the beads were arranged to make up these motifs is made BELOW. *c.* 1361 – 1352 BC.

65 The use of nets of cylinder beads over a plain tunic is illustrated RIGHT. Dresses completely covered in bead patterns – usually taking the form of the design shown TOP LEFT, sometimes occur on wall-paintings. Variations on this simple formula are very common as, for instance, in the examples from objects in Tutankhamun's tomb BELOW.

66 Designs based on interlocking circles are also found among the painted ceiling patterns. The design BOTTOM is an oddity, however, and best drawn – with difficulty – on a square grid. The gridwork is not original.

67 Other ceiling patterns based on circles are typically arranged in rows without interlocking. Note the lotus-and-bud motif which makes up the roundels in the pattern CENTRE and the combined lily/palmette motif BOTTOM. The gridwork is not original.

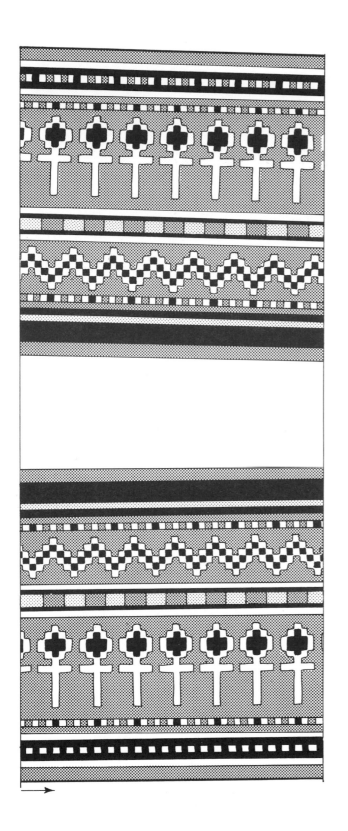

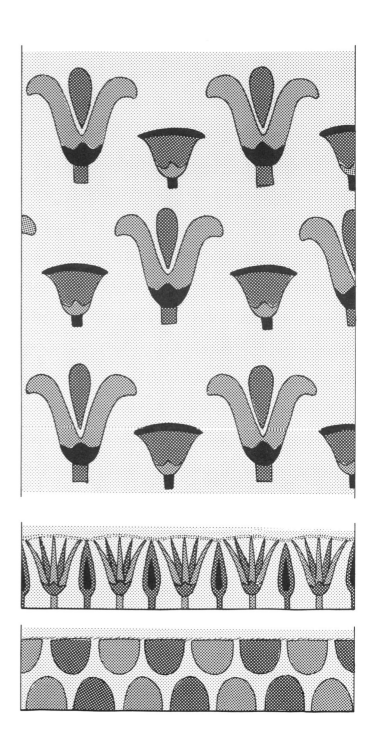

68 LEFT Detail of the design from the 'Girdle of Ramesses III' (*c.* 1198 – 1166 BC). The 5.2 m long sash is in double warp-face weave (the arrow indicates the direction of the warp). RIGHT The over-all design of lilies and papyrus and the borders of a tapestry-woven cloth in the tomb of Tuthmosis IV (*c.* 1425 – 1417 BC).

69 Details from wall-paintings. TOP The upright loom was introduced in the New Kingdom. It was used to weave large cloths and tapestry. BOTTOM The ground loom on the Middle Kingdom tomb-painting is shown in the aspective convention. The warp-face woven bands of 68 and 71 could have been produced on this type of loom. The girl RIGHT is plying yarn from two threads.

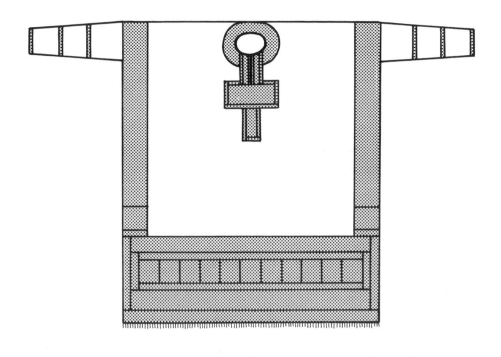

70 One of the tunics found in Tutankhamun's tomb. It is of fine linen with woven and embroidered applied bands (their position is indicated ABOVE). BELOW is a reconstruction of two of the embroidered panels. Their condition is poor, but outline and chain stitch have been recognised. *c.* 1361 – 1352 BC.

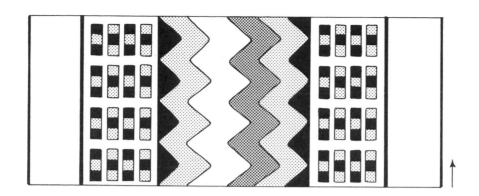

71 Design of warp-face weave linen bands from the tunic OPPOSITE (the arrows indicate the direction of the warp). The colours are difficult to distinguish with certainty: black indicates black, dark blue or brown, the dark screen red or brown and the light screen pale blue or grey.

72 On the tomb-paintings, foreign visitors are often shown in patterned clothes while the Egyptians wear only white. TOP A group of Semitic travellers dressed in clothes of dyed wool or appliquéd leather. BOTTOM Designs from kilts worn by Cretan princes. Patterns like these influenced Egyptian art (see 74).

73 Wooden 'dolls', found in tombs, probably represent Nubian concubines. Their patterned dresses are painted in black, red and green; the hair is represented by strings of clay beads. *c.* 2040 – 2000 BC.

74 LEFT and CENTRE Influences from the Minoan cultures in the Aegean can be seen in the interlocking spiral scrolls of these ceiling patterns from the Middle Kingdom.

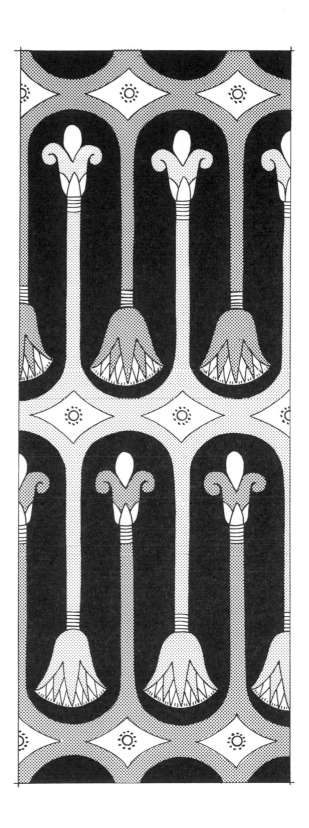

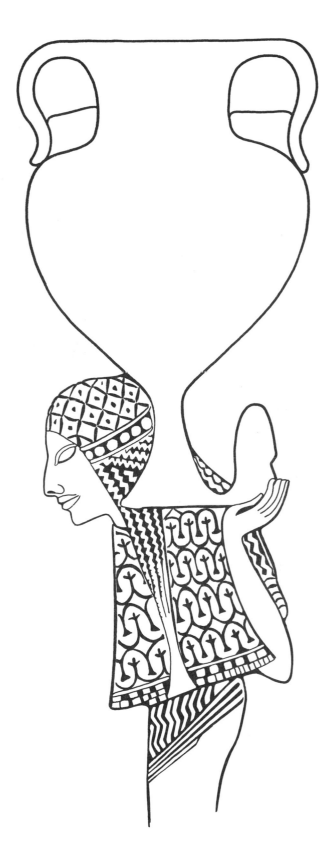

75 The interlocking arcading, combined with the lotus and papyrus motifs on the ceiling patterns LEFT and OPPOSITE RIGHT, is also the design on the girl's cloak on a fragmentary cosmetic spoon of wood RIGHT.

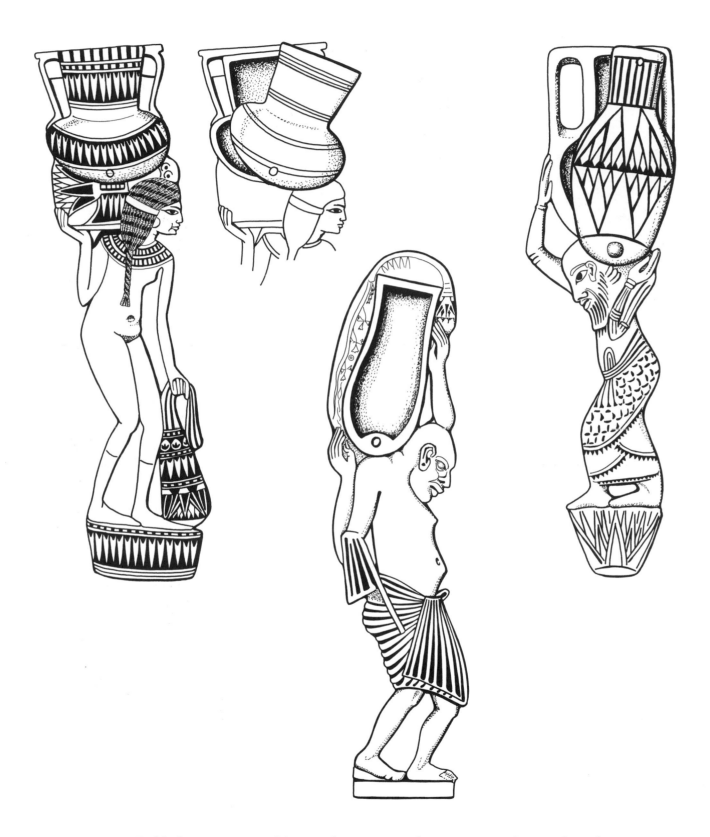

76 Lidded spoons carved in wood are among the most attractive artefacts from ancient Egypt. They are thought to have contained ointment and other substances for cosmetic use, but some may have been used in the temples for ritual purposes.

77 These elaborately carved cosmetic spoons are inlaid with coloured paste. They are from the 18th Dynasty of the New Kingdom (*c.* 1400 – 1320 BC).

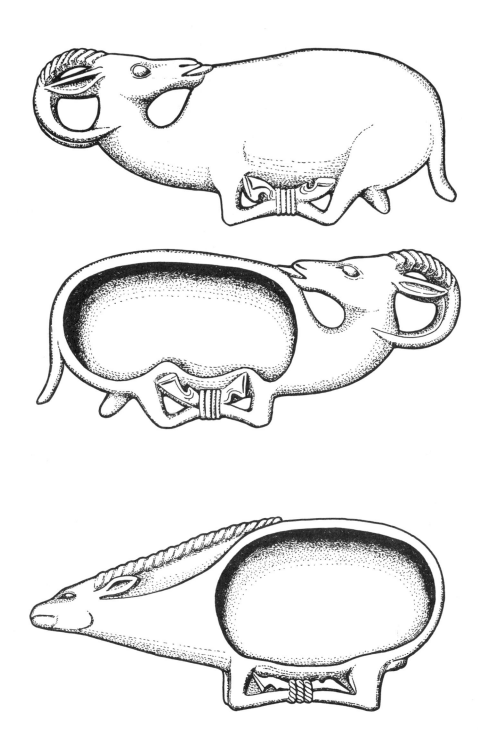

78 TOP Both sides of a cosmetic spoon carved in wood. The spoon of similar design BELOW is of blue glazed composition.

79 Carved cosmetic spoons inlaid with coloured paste. All the typical plant motifs are present here: lotus-and-bud, papyrus, lily/palmette, rosette, mandrake fruit etc.

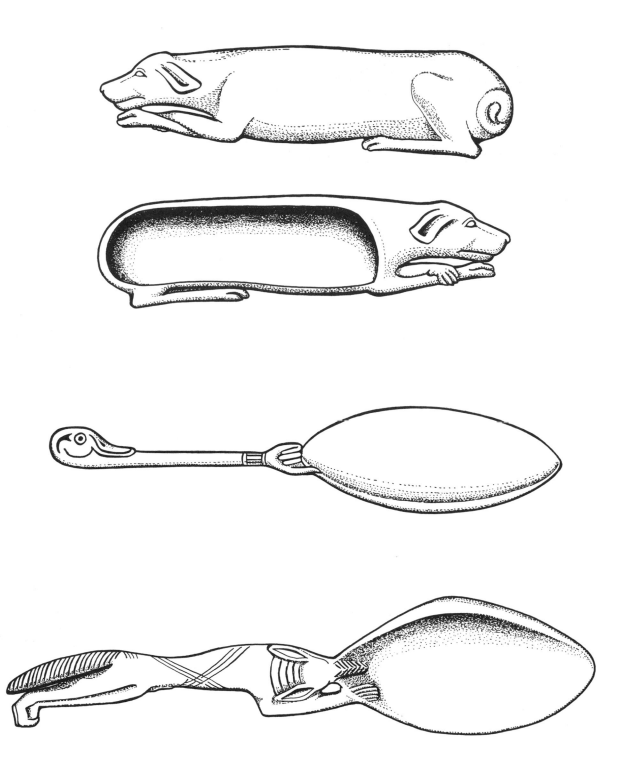

80 TOP Both sides of a cosmetic spoon carved in ivory. The bowls of the spoons BELOW are in the shape of shells. The duck's head handle terminal is a very common motif.

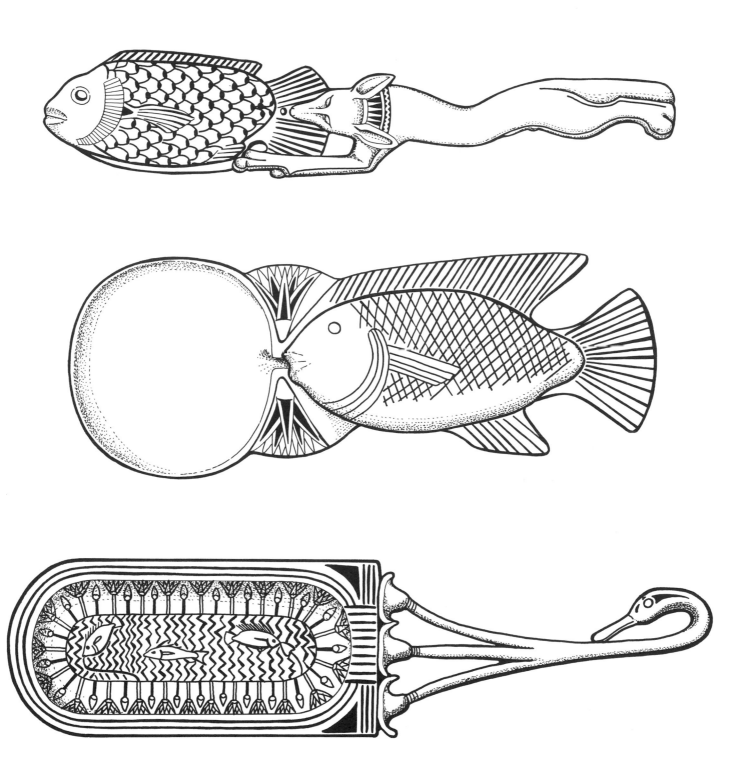

81 Cosmetic spoons carved in wood and inlaid with coloured paste. TOP The body of the fish is a lid which covers the bowl of the spoon. The body of the fish, CENTRE, is also a lid covering a space which connects with the open bowl through the mouth of the fish.

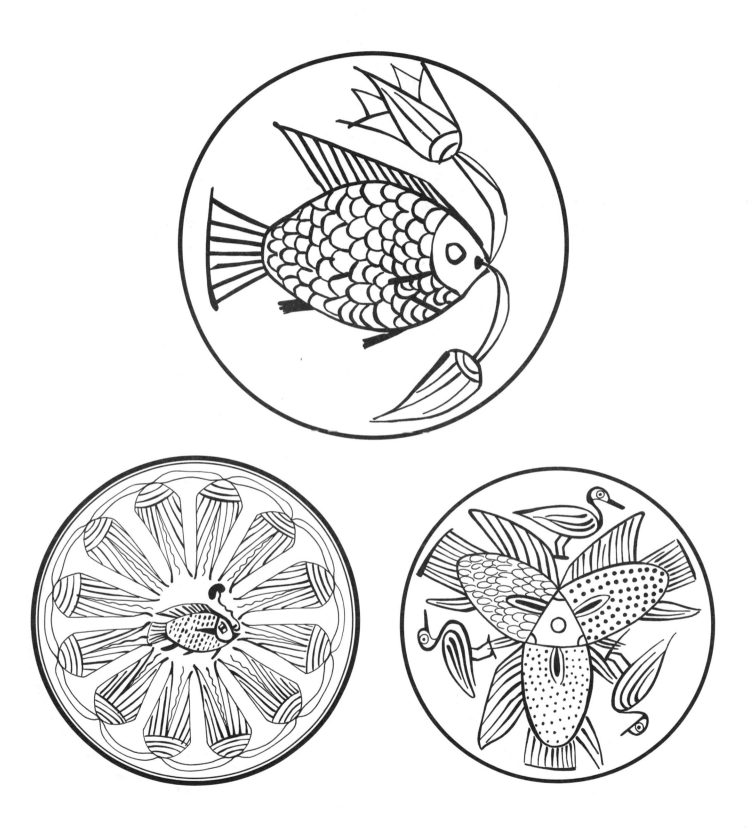

82 While pottery was undecorated, glazed composition ware was painted with lively and attractive designs. Illustrated here are such designs painted in black inside blue glazed bowls. The outsides often have simple patterns of lotus petals radiating from the base. All date from the New Kingdom.

83 The motif of ponds with fish and water plants often occurs on these bowls. The fish *Tilapia nilotica* hatches its eggs in the mouth, from which they swim fully formed; it thus became a symbol of the creative force.

84 While the decoration TOP simply represents the good life, the motif BOTTOM is the goddess Hathor, represented as a cow, or a woman with cow's ears. She is often shown wearing a horned headdress (*see* 86).

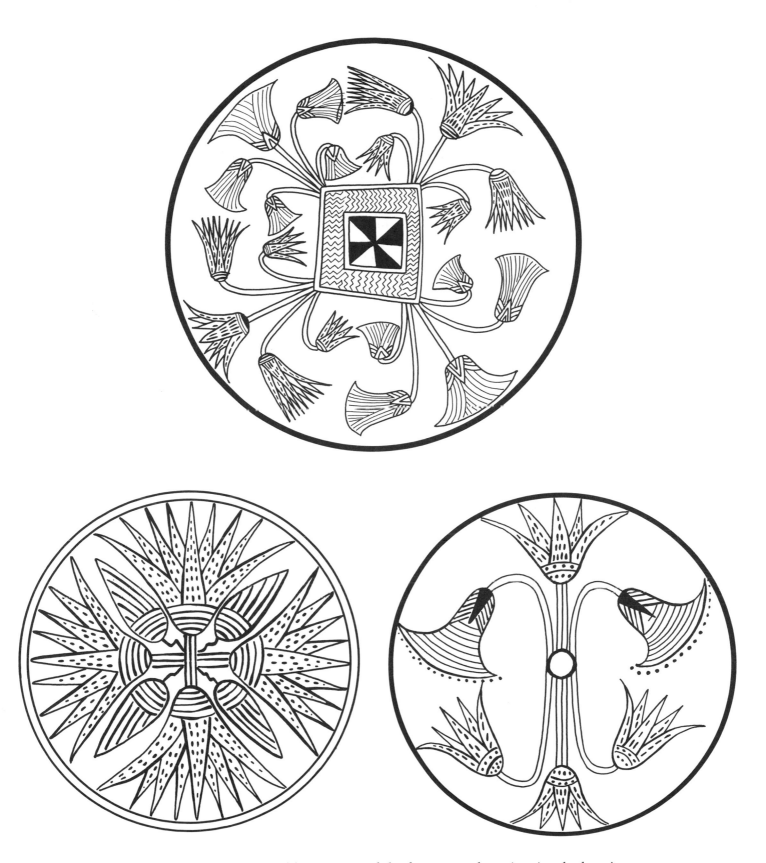

85 The square pond TOP adds tension and rhythm to an otherwise simple drawing of lotus and papyrus. The common lotus-and-bud motif LEFT is here nicely given added interest by the oval shape created at the centre of the round bowl. A well-judged sparing design is shown RIGHT.

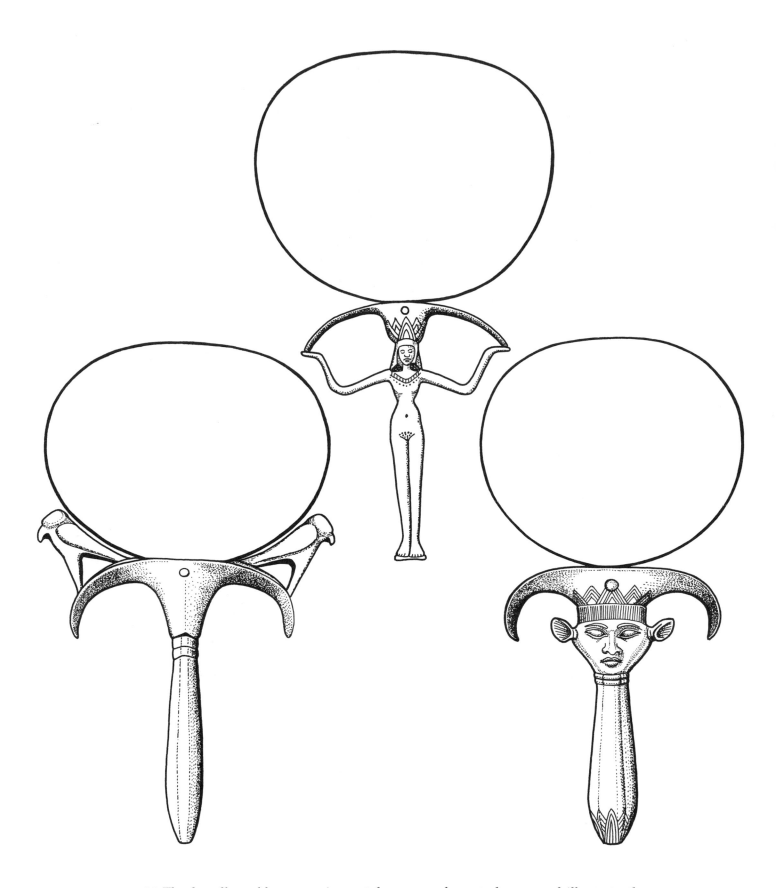

86 The handles of bronze mirrors take many elegant shapes and illustrate the sure instinct for proportion and form of the Egyptian craftsman.

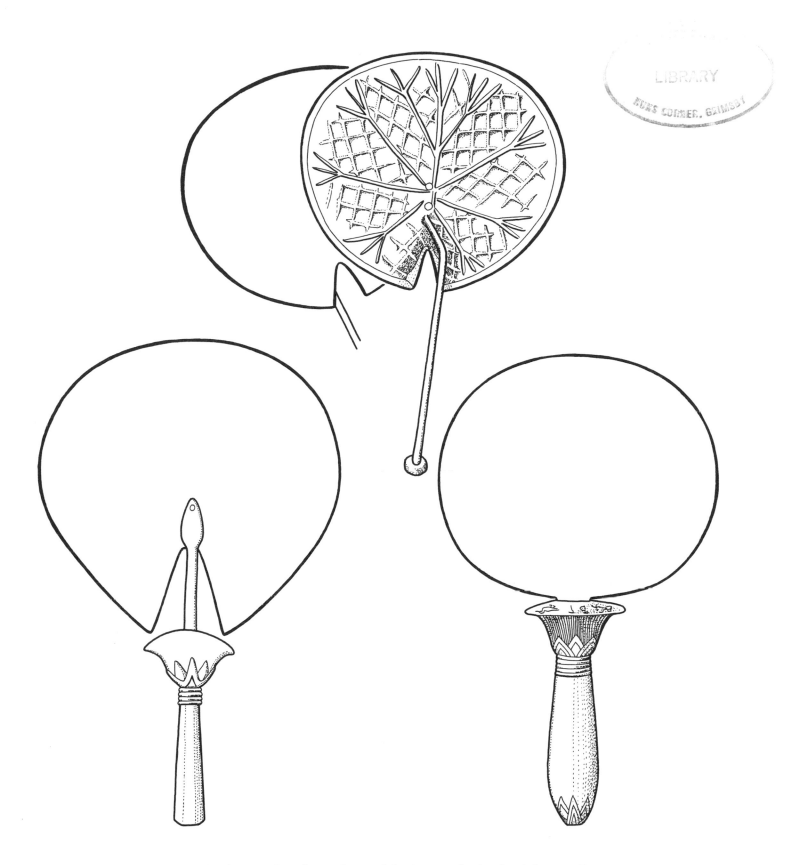

87 The lotus leaf is used in the embossed design on the back of the small mirror TOP (approx. actual size) from *c.* 1300 BC and on the mirror LEFT. The papyrus-shaped handle of the earlier mirror RIGHT from the Middle Kingdom (*c.* 1900 BC) is of blue glazed composition and carries the name of the owner in hieroglyphs.

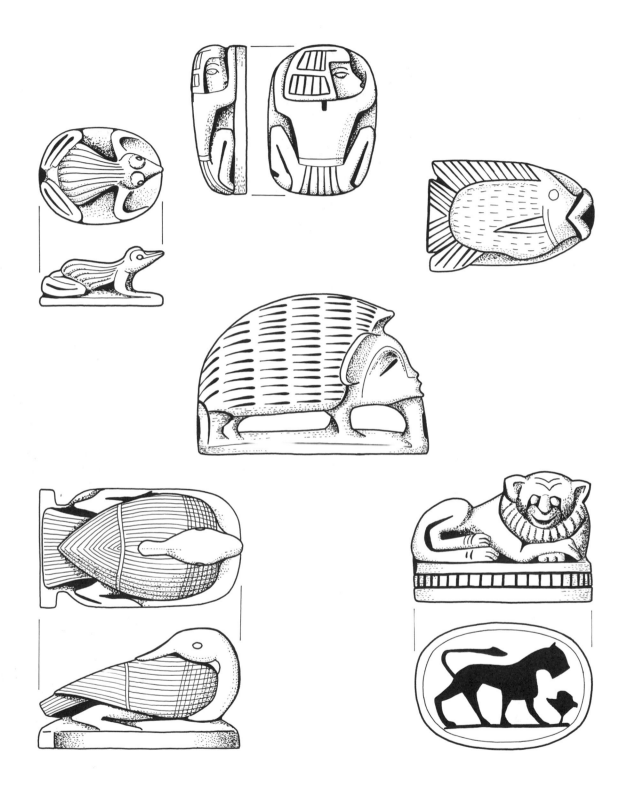

88 The Egyptians had no locks and small seals were pressed into lumps of soft clay to secure the owner's possessions. Such seals are known from the beginning of the Dynastic Period onwards and are found in very large numbers. The earliest examples are of a variety of shapes. Approx. 3:1.

89 The seal of the ordinary person was usually very small – typically between one and three centimetres long. Only the decorated backs of seals are shown in these pages, except TOP LEFT, BOTTOM RIGHT and OPPOSITE BOTTOM RIGHT where the seal design is also illustrated. Approx. 3:1.

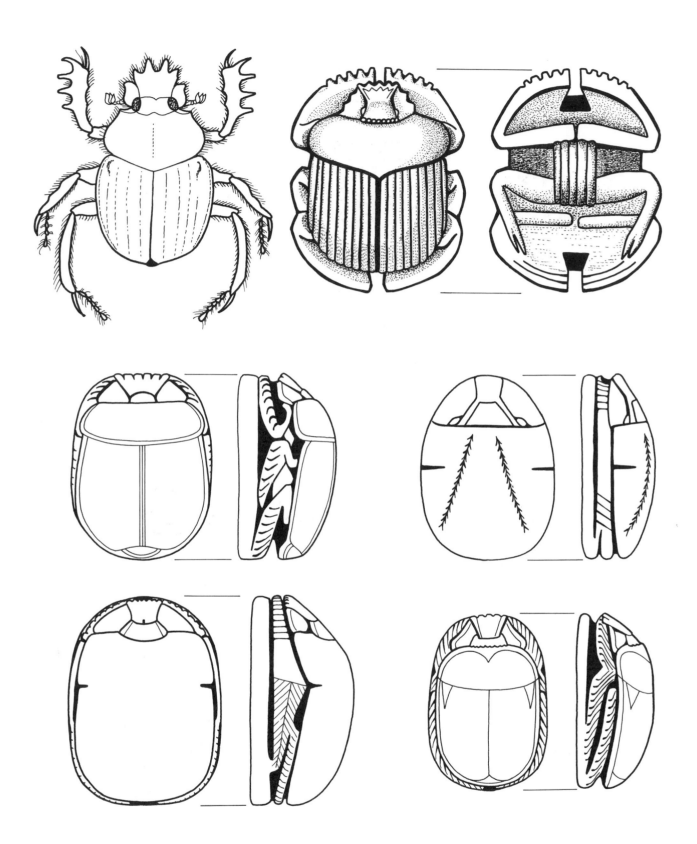

90 From the Middle Kingdom onwards the majority of seals take the form of the familiar scarab beetle with the seal design engraved on the underside. TOP LEFT *Scarabaeus sacer* L. was the most important species to be used. RIGHT an amulet which realistically renders this beetle (2:1). BELOW a few examples of scarab seal backs. Approx. 3:1.

91 Early seal designs are simple geometric and 'maze' patterns which may have developed from designs of stick animals and human figures. A crouching animal can be distinguished in the design BOTTOM LEFT. Approx. 3:1.

92 Scroll patterns made up of interlocking spirals are old motifs which were probably developed in Egypt from plant ornament. The earliest examples are simple, but the motif developed into designs of unlimited potential for variation, skilfully adapted to the small fields of the seals. These examples are of continuous interlocking scrolls. Approx. 3:1.

93 In these examples the scrolls have a beginning and an end. These patterns are also associated with plant motifs (98). Approx. 3:1.

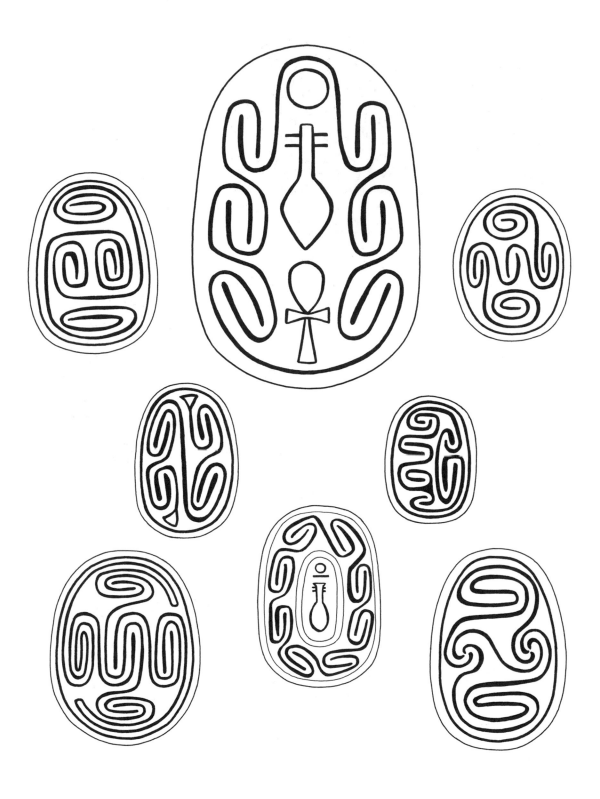

94 A flattened scroll is another variation on the same theme. These are particularly frequently used as a frame round signs of symbolic significance. The examples CENTRE contain the signs of the sun, life and good luck. Approx. 3:1.

95 Concentric circles, produced mechanically, became a popular motif on seals. They occur both as the primary motif and in conjunction with others (97, 100). Approx. 3:1.

96 Coiled and interlaced designs. Approx. 3:1.

97 Knotted and interlaced designs. The knot is a separate motif and does not always form part of the interlace (100). Approx. 3:1.

98 The common plant motifs, lotus, papyrus and sedge, frequently occur on the seals. Approx. 3:1.

99 The earliest animal and human motifs are simple, but they become more elaborate in later periods. The fish motif is here, as in Egyptian art generally, very common, while other animal motifs may have a heraldic significance. Approx. 3:1.

100 The division of the field into quarters to form a floral cross is a later motif. Some of the leaf shapes can be distinguished as the debased uraeus, or cobra, sign which had royal connotations. The symbolic signs which occur on many seals emphasize their role as helpful amulets apart from their practical use.